UFOS IN THE QURAN

Abdul Aziz Khan

Strategic Book Publishing
New York, New York

Strategic Book Publishing

An imprint of AEG Publishing Group

845 Third Avenue, 6th Floor - 6016

New York, NY 10022

www.StrategicBookPublishing.com

ISBN 978-1-60693-158-5   1-60693-158-X

Printed in the United States of America

Book Design: Linda W. Rigsbee

Dedication

To my parents

Contents

Foreword

Science fiction and theological surmise make a heady mix. It could quickly degenerate into pseudo cosmology ridden away into the wild blue yonder by a chariot of the gods. However, this is not the case in this fine and well-researched offering of Abdul Aziz. He is not hallucinating nor is he wandering in a world devoid of supporting dimensions. He has walked a tight rope between fiction and faith and placed before us his findings.

I was overwhelmed when he asked me to write this foreword. I make no claims to being a religious scholar, nor do I stock too many books by Arthur C. Clark or movies by Steven Spielberg in my library. Yet, like any other terrestrial mortal I have looked at the stars, gazed with wonder at the celestial dance of the cosmos, and have been a student of the history of time. In short, I too have walked along the path of unanswered questions and been puzzled at how little we actually know. The secrets are "His." We grow curiouser and curiouser with time, and despite scientific breakthroughs and advancement of knowledge, we grudgingly accept that the secrets of "the book" will be revealed slowly and methodically at "His" choosing. Abdul Aziz probably chose me because I seem to attract controversy. He is the one who is letting the genii out of the bottle, not me. His wish was my command.

Read, think, accept, or reject—the book will stir all sorts of emotions in you. Perhaps some of what you read will help you to

understand what we call, in a facile manner, the supernatural.
Reality is closer to you than your jugular vein.

Imran Aslam

Karachi

PART I

Secret History of the UFO Phenomenon

The Second World War ended with the emergence of the United States and Soviet Union as two super powers locked in a violent struggle for global domination. It was during this Cold War period (1945 to 1989) that certain mysterious and bizarre incidents took place in different parts of the world. Had the governments of those concerned regions openly shared these incidents with their populations, our understanding of Islam would be very different today. But as part of a global censorship plan, this information was buried in the top-secret intelligence files of these super powers. For decades, it remained buried and it was maintained by these two Cold War rivals assuming that any leakage of this information would constitute a direct threat to their national security.

Before we examine Islamic scriptures and their connection to recently discovered UFO phenomenon, it is necessary to look at this "secret history" that has been kept hidden from the world. The following four chapters contain information that is necessary in order to understand certain passages of Islamic scriptures.

CHAPTER 1

ORIGIN OF THE FASTWALKERS

The U.S. Government's Secret Research into UFOs

Humankind is being monitored from outer space. Orbiting the earth at an altitude of 23,750 miles, are seven satellites that look down upon us continuously. With their 6,144 sound sensors, they can not only pick up the movement of conventional aircrafts, but are also capable of locating meteorites coming toward the earth from outer space. Positioned geo-synchronously, they have every inch of the earth's surface covered around the clock. There is not a spot on the earth where you can hide from them. They are America's eyes in the sky!

Lee Graham and Ron Regehr, two engineers who had worked for Aerojet (the company that developed the Deep Space Program [DSP]), revealed that since the time they were launched, these space platforms began detecting a specific type of flying object that could not be classified in conventional terms. It was no aircraft, nor was it any kind of meteorite. It would come from outer space at lightning speeds, enter the earth's atmosphere, and then return to its cosmic origin after a fixed period of time. According to the two engineers, DSP satellites spotted these objects an average of two to three times per month.[1] They were given the name "Fastwalkers."

On September 19, 1976, DSP satellites picked up a Fastwalker over the Middle East. Within minutes of its entry into the earth's atmosphere, it was detected by the radar of the Iranian Air Force base, "Shahroki." At once, two F-4 Phantoms of the Royal Iranian Air Force took off from the airbase to intercept the intruder. Iranian pilots were able to see it from a distance of seventy nautical miles. It was a gigantic disk that was brightly lit by multicolored lights. As one of the F-4s came close to the object, the electronic instruments on board stopped functioning. Immediately, the radio contact was lost and the pilot had no choice but to abort the mission.

The pilot of the second aircraft witnessed a strange phenomenon. He observed a smaller object come out of the larger disc and fly toward him. When he attempted to fire, the firing panel of the aircraft went dead and he too lost radio contact with the base. He also aborted the mission and managed to land safely. The small UFO returned to the gigantic disc and, in a few hours, the same UFO was spotted over the skies of Morocco.

The story made the news the next day. Teheran-based newspapers reported the incident based on the information provided to them by the air force.[2] On the orders of Shah Reza Pahlevi, the ruler of Iran at the time, the Royal Iranian Air Force prepared a detailed report of the incident and forwarded a copy to the U. S. Embassy in Teheran. A copy of this report is presented on the following page:

---

[1] Hesseman, preface xviii
[2] UFOs the Secret History, p. 319

This report forwards information regarding the sightings of a UFO in Iran on September 19, 1976.

A.   At about 12:30 a.m. on 19th Sep 76, ___ (words here are blacked out in the original document) received 4 telephone calls from citizens living in the Shemiran area of Teheran saying that they had seen objects in the sky. Some reported a kind of birdlike object, while others reported a helicopter with a light on. There were no helicopters airborne at that time. ___ (blacked)

After he had told the citizen it was only stars and had talked to Mehrabad Tower, he decided to look for himself. He noticed an object in the sky similar to a star, bigger and brighter. He decided to scramble an F-4 from Shahroki AFB to investigate.

B.   At 1:30 on the 19th, the F-4 took off and proceeded to a point about 40 nautical miles north of Tehran. Due to its brilliance, the object was easily visible from 70 miles away. As the F-4 approached a range of 25 nm, he lost all instrumentation and communication (UHF and Intercom). He broke off the intercept and headed back for Shahroki. When the F-4 turned away from the object, and apparently was no longer a threat to it, the aircraft regained all instrumentation and communications. At 1:40, a second F-4 was launched. The back-seater acquired a radar lock on at 27 nm and a 12 o'clock high position with VC (rate of closure) at 150 nmph. As the range decreased to 25 nm, the object moved away at a speed that was visible on the radar scope and stayed at 25 nm.

C.   The size of the radar return was comparable to that of a 707 tanker. The visual size of the object was difficult to discern because of its brilliance. The light that it gave off was that of flashing strobe lights arranged in rectangular pattern and alternating blue, green, red, and orange in color. The sequence of the lights was so fast that all the colors could be seen at once. The object and the pursuing F-4 continued to a course to the south of Tehran, when another brightly lit object, estimated to be one half to one third the apparent size of the moon, came out of the original object. The second object headed straight toward the F-4 at a very fast rate of speed. The pilot attempted to fire an AIM-9 missile at the object, but at that instant, his weapons control panel went off and he lost all communications (UHF and interphone). At this point, the pilot initiated a turn and a negative G dive to get away. As he continued in his turn away from the primary object, the secondary object went to the inside of his turn, and then returned to the primary object for a perfect rejoin.

D.   Shortly after the second object joined up with the primary object, another object appeared to come out of the other side of the first object going straight down at a great rate of speed. The F-4 crew had regained communications and control of the weapons panel, and they watched the object approach the ground anticipating a large explosion. This object appeared to come to rest gently on the earth and cast a very bright light over an area of about 2 miles.

The crew descended from their altitude of 26 M to 15 M and continued to observe and mark the object's position. They had some difficulty in adjusting their night visibility for landing, so after circling Mehrabad a few times, they went in for a straight landing. There was a lot of interference on the UHF and each time they passed through a magnetic bearing of 150 degrees from Mehrabad, they lost their communication (UHF and interphone), and the INS fluctuated between 30 to 50 degrees. The one civil airliner that was approaching Mehrabad during this time experienced communications failure in the same vicinity (Kilo Zulu), but did not report seeing anything. While the F-4 was on a long, final approach, the crew noticed another cylinder-shaped object about the size of a T-bird at 10 M with bright, steady lights on each end and a flasher in the middle. When queried, the tower stated there was no other traffic in the area. During the time the object passed over the F-4, the tower did not have a visual on it but picked it up after the pilot told them to look between the mountains and the refinery.

E.   During the daylight, the F-4 crew was taken out to the area in a helicopter where the object had apparently landed. Nothing was noticed at the spot where they thought the object landed (a dry lake bed), but as they circled off to the west of the area they picked up a very noticeable beeper signal. At the point where the return was the loudest, there was a small house with a garden. They landed and asked the people there if they had noticed anything strange last night. The people talked about a loud noise and a very bright light like lightning. The aircraft and the area where the object is believed to have landed are being checked for possible radiation. More information will be forwarded when it becomes available.

The U.S. Embassy in Iran forwarded this report to the White House, the State Department, CIA, DIA, NSA, and the Joint Chiefs of Staff at the Pentagon. Commanders of U.S. forces in the Middle East were also provided a copy. An incident of this level should have been in the news all around the globe. Instead, it was buried in the secret files of the CIA along with hundreds of other similar reports collected from different parts of the world.[3]

This is not the only UFO-related report that is now available to the public. A large number of previously classified documents have been released under the Freedom of Information Act (FOIA). These provide considerable evidence that the U.S. government carried out investigations into some sort of unexplained, aerial phenomenon, and that the results of these investigations are being withheld. From some of the documents that have leaked out, UFO researchers have tried to fit together the information to form a complete picture. Since all parts of this "jigsaw puzzle" have not come out yet, a complete picture has not yet emerged. From whatever little information

---

[3] Hesseman, pp. 319-321

is available, it can be established that the very first UFO report came in on Tuesday, June 24, 1947, from private pilot Kenneth Arnold.

The First Reported UFO Sighting (1947)

On Tuesday, June 24, 1947, Kenneth Arnold, a thirty-two-year-old pilot, started the engines of his private aircraft. Earlier on, an air force C-46 transport aircraft was reported missing in the region and a $5,000 reward was set for the person who found the plane. The reward tempted Arnold and he decided to spend an hour in the air looking for the lost plane. Arnold was an experienced pilot who did forty to one hundred flying hours a month. He was also experienced in flying over mountains at low altitudes, and he had an aircraft that was particularly suited for that purpose. He took off from Chihalis, Washington, at about 2:00 p.m. and an hour later he was flying over the Mount Rainer region. While searching the slopes and high plateaus for the lost aircraft, he was distracted by a quick beam of light that reflected on the side of his plane. His first reaction was to think that he was on a collision course with another aircraft whose presence he had not noticed. But other than a DC-4 flying miles away on the horizon, there was no aircraft in sight. Suddenly, a second flash of light caught his eye. This time he saw them clearly.

There were nine of them flying one after another in a row formation. First, Arnold thought that they were fighter planes, but as they came closer, he noticed that they had no wings, no tails, or any other projecting parts. A bluish-white light radiated out from their upper surface and they flew at a speed unusual for aircrafts of that time. The formation quickly passed Mt. Adams and disappeared over the horizon. The sighting had lasted only three minutes and the formation had covered an unusually great distance in such a short duration. Arnold estimated that the formation was five miles long and, within 102 seconds, it had covered a distance of fifty miles. This was an unbelievable speed of 1700 to 2000 miles an hour.

At the Cascade Mountains, not far from where Kenneth Arnold had seen the objects, an old gold digger from Oregon spotted the nine objects in the sky. He was carrying a compass and as the formation flew past him, his compass went crazy. It seemed as if the presence of the objects interfered directly with the magnetic principles that made the compass work.

Arnold returned to base and reported to the press what became known as "The First UFO Sighting of the Modern Age." "They were flat as a plate and so smooth that they reflected the sun like a mirror. You can call me Einstein or Flash Gordon or just a nut, but I know what I saw. The things flew like saucers when you make them skip over water," Arnold stated at a press conference. It was this comparison of unidentified flying objects with the motion of "saucers skipping over water" that gave birth to the term "flying saucers."

The press was convinced that they had a story that would make headlines. Arnold had been a Boy Scout in high school, was chosen by the state of Minnesota to take part in the Olympics, and had a lifesaver certificate in swimming. In college, he was a successful football player. Later on he worked as a salesman for fire extinguishers with the firm Red Comet, and established his own business in the field two years later. He acquired his pilot license at an early age, and since then had made deliveries to his customers by plane. His father was a prominent local politician and a close associate of Senator Burton K. Wheeler. Arnold was more than what journalists understood as a "credible witness." Thus, the newspapers covered Arnold's encounter and in the days to come the term "flying saucers" was repeated in the news everywhere; it was a term no one knew before Kenneth Arnold's sighting

First UFO Photographs Appear in Newspaper

On July 7, 1947, William Rhodes of Phoenix, Arizona, an amateur photographer, stepped out of his house and headed toward his workshop when he heard the sound of a fighter aircraft approaching at low altitude. Thinking that it was a perfect opportunity to photograph a low-flying plane, he rushed inside and got his camera. Back outside, what he saw in the air was no aircraft. It was an almost circular object with no tail, no wings, no projections, and had a small light radiating from its rear. Rhodes took two pictures before the object finally disappeared in the clouds. He developed the photographs in his own dark room, and two days later they appeared in the local newspaper, *The Arizona Republic*, under the headline "Saucer Flies in the Sky at Unbelievable Speeds."

When Kenneth Arnold saw the photographs, he was convinced that these were genuine because they resembled very closely what he had seen over Mount Rainer a month before. He had not disclosed the details of their physical appearance so accurately to the press for them to make up the pictures. Thirty years later, a UFO investigation group, Saucer Watch, examined these photos using computerized, state-of-the-art technology. The photograph turned out to be genuine. The investigation confirmed that the object photographed was 30 to 36 feet in diameter and no less than 4,500 feet from the camera when it was photographed.

While it was through William Rhodes' photographs that most people saw a UFO for the first time, these pictures were not the first UFO photographs ever. The very first photograph of a UFO had already been taken fifty-nine years before in 1883. Jose Bonilla, a Mexican astronomer and the head of Zacatecus observatory in Paris, had photographed a series of UFOs while watching the sun through his telescope. Two years later in 1885, these photographs had appeared in a magazine called *L'Astronomie.*

As far as William Rhodes' photos were concerned, the FBI appeared within forty-eight hours of the publication of his photographs. Rhodes was interrogated by Mr. Ledding, a civil official, and Lt. Col. Beam from the air force. They confiscated the negatives and assured Rhodes that he would get them back soon. This never happened! Instead, the negatives were forwarded to the Air Material Command (AMC), the intelligence service of the air force.

The Twining Memorandum

By September 1947, the AMC had gathered 156 reports of UFO sightings, 117 of which could not be classified as conventional aircraft or any natural weather phenomenon. No rational explanation could be given regarding their origin, thus the AMC reports classified them as "unidentified." At the time of the Pentagon's request for the AMC's opinion regarding these "flying saucers," the intelligence service was headed by Second World War's famous Chief of Staff, General Nathan F. Twining. Based on the reports collected by the AMC, General Twining forwarded a top secret report to Brig. Gen. George Schulgen at the Pentagon. This report stated the following:

1. As requested by AC/AS-2, presented below is the considered opinion of this command concerning the so-called "Flying Discs." This opinion is based on interrogatory report data furnished by AC/AS-2, preliminary studies by personnel of T-2 and Aircraft Laboratory, and Engineering Division T-3. This opinion was arrived at in a conference between personnel from the Air Institute of Technology, Intelligence T-2 Office, Chief of Engineering Division and the Aircraft, Power Plant, and Propeller Laboratories of Engineering Division T-3.

2. It is the opinion that:

    a. The phenomenon reported is something real and not visionary or fictitious.

    b. There are objects probably approximating the shape of a disc, of such appreciable size as to appear to be as large as man-made aircraft.

    c. There is a possibility that some of the incidents may be caused by natural phenomenon, such as meteors.

    d. The reported operating characteristics such as extreme rates of climb, maneuverability (particularly in roll), and action which must be considered evasive when sighted or contacted by friendly aircraft and radar, lend belief to the possibility that some of the objects are controlled either manually or remotely.

    e. The apparent common description of the objects is as follows:

        1.) Metallic or light-reflecting surface.

        2.) Absence of trail, except in few instances when the object apparently was operating under high performance conditions.

        3.) Circular and elliptical in shape, flat on bottom, and domed on top.

        4.) Several reports of well-kept formation flights varying from three to nine objects.

        5.) Normally no associated sound, except in three instances a substantial rumbling roar was noted.

        6.) Level flight speeds normally above 300 knots are estimated.

f.   It is possible that with current technical knowledge- provided extensive detailed development is undertaken-the U.S. could construct a piloted aircraft according to the general description of the object in subparagraph (e) which would be capable of flying at an approximate range of 7000 miles at subsonic speeds.

g.   Any development in this country along the lines indicated in (f) would be extremely expensive, time consuming, and would considerably take away from current projects, and therefore, if undertaken, should be set up independent of existing projects.

h.   Due consideration must be given to the following:

1.)   The possibility that these objects are of domestic origin- the product of some high-security project not known to the AC/AS-2 or this Command.

2.)   The lack of physical evidence in case of crash-recovered exhibits which would undeniably prove the existence of these objects.

3.)   The possibility that some foreign nation has a form of propulsion, possibly nuclear, which is outside our domestic knowledge.

3.   It is recommended that:

a.   Headquarters, Army Air Force issue a directive assigning a priority, security classification, and Code Name for a detailed study of this material. This should include the preparation of complete sets of all available and pertinent data which then will be made available to the army, navy, Atomic Energy Commission, JRDB, the Air Force Scientific Advisory Group, NACA, the RAND, and NEPA projects. This would be for comments and recommendations with a preliminary report to be forwarded within 15 days of receipt of the data, and a detailed report thereafter every 30 days as the investigation develops. Data should be completely interchanged.

4.   Awaiting a specific directive, AMC will continue the investigation within its current resources in order to more closely define the nature of the phenomenon.

Detailed Essential Elements of Information will be formulated immediately for transmittal through channels.

    N. F. TWINING

    Lieutenant General, USA Commander

For thirty-one years, this document, officially known as the Twining Memorandum, was withheld from the public and was finally released under U.S. President Jimmy Carter.

The U.S. Government's First UFO Investigation

The Twining Memorandum had established that flying discs were real. The only point that remained was whether they were of Russian or extraterrestrial origin. Thus in autumn 1947, there began the American government's first attempt to solve the UFO mystery. Military authorities decided that they would start tracking UFO activity at the poles, for it was assumed that in case of Russian spy planes, the polar region would be the shortest route and for extraterrestrial spacecrafts, Earth's magnetic field and radiation belts still made it the best place to enter the planet's atmosphere.

In the autumn of 1947, B-29 Bombers were modified to make 12-16 hour reconnaissance flights. Initially, they were fitted with 16 mm film cameras, which were later replaced by 25 mm, and finally with a 70 mm camera provided by Wright Field. Still pictures were to be taken by Fairchild K-20 cameras, which produced 8 x 8 negatives. Besides film and still cameras, the planes were also fitted with special emission scanners that were capable of picking up radio frequency fields, isolating and recording them for thirty seconds, and then scanning again to monitor any changes that had occurred during that time.

The leader of the project was Captain Wendelle C. Stevens. Stevens had graduated from the military academy in 1942 and had served as a test pilot. In 1945, he received training in aeronautic technology at the Wright Field Air Force Base in Dayton, Ohio. Later on, he was assigned to the Foreign Technology Division of the Air Intelligence. For this special mission, he was transferred to Fort Richardson, Alaska, and was told that the aim of this mission was to observe and record meteorological phenomenon. He was to look for anything unusual, film or photograph it, and then send his report with films and photographs to the AMC. It was also his job to brief the crew, make them swear to secrecy, and finally debrief them after every mission. It soon became clear to Stevens that what the air force was looking for in the skies wasn't any weather phenomenon, but something more sinister.

The pilots who flew these missions returned with stories of flying discs that were capable of traveling at enormous speeds. They could stop in midair, stand still, and shoot off in any direction making sharp G-turns. They were unlike any aircraft these pilots had seen until then, and in certain cases in which the discs flew fairly close to the aircrafts, their presence caused changes in the navigational instruments on board. During these reconnaissance flights, some of the UFOs had also been caught on tape. This provided the AMC with not only detailed reports, but also the very first film footage showing the unusual flight characteristics of the "flying saucers."[4]

The Pentagon and AMC analyzed these reports and, toward the end of the year, the United States Defense Department was split into

---

[4] Hesseman, pp. 36-37

two factions holding two different views regarding the nature and origins of the flying discs. One faction remained convinced that flying discs were Soviet surveillance probes or spy planes. The other strongly believed that the development of such a technology was far beyond the ability of the Soviet Union or any other terrestrial power; they were intruders from outer space.

Saucer Kills Air Force Pilot

On January 7, 1948, at 2:45 p.m., a gigantic flying saucer was reported over Godman Air Force Base in Kentucky. Colonel Hix, who was commander of the air force base at Godman, dispatched three aircrafts to intercept it. The leader of this squadron was an experienced pilot, Capt. Thomas Mantell. The three pilots pursued the gigantic flying disc, but two of them had to land when they ran out of fuel. The third one, Capt. Mantell himself, continued to chase it. Throughout the chase, Capt. Mantell maintained radio contact with the base and, in the radio conversation, he described the object as "metallic" and "tremendous in size." The pilot further stated that he was going up to 20,000 feet to get a closer look at the object, which was gaining altitude as Mantell approached it. Mantell's plane was not equipped with an oxygen supply, which was needed at altitudes above 15,000 feet. As he flew above that level to get a closer look, he started blacking out. At 3:15 p.m., the jet crashed and the pilot was killed. The disc continued to fly and two hours later, at around 5:15 p.m. it was sighted over Lockburne Airport in Ohio.

Investigations into the crash revealed that the pilot's watch had stopped exactly at 3:10 p.m. and, at the very last second, the pilot had put his aircraft in a steep dive probably to reach a breathable altitude as quickly as possible. Captain Thomas Mantell became the first American casualty caused by a "flying saucer."[5]

The Pentagon reacted quickly. So far, flying discs had been an unexplained phenomenon, but now concerns rose whether they constituted a direct threat to the security of the United States. Major General L.C. Craigie gave orders for the initiation of an air force project to determine whether these flying discs were a threat to the national security of the United States. This project, which began on January 22, 1948, was code named Project SIGN.

The finest experts were selected to lead the project and it was assigned the second highest priority level of 2A. During the next thirteen months, Project SIGN investigated 240 sightings within the United States and thirty outside of it. About 30 percent of these cases could be explained as deliberate hoaxes, weather phenomenon, conventional aircrafts, optical illusions, etc. For the remaining 70 percent, neither the investigators nor the AMC had any explanation. Since the word "flying saucer" had become ludicrous because of its reckless use by the media, the term "unidentified flying object" or "UFO" was adopted.[6] While most incidents Project SIGN investigated came from credible sources, such as high-ranking military officials, astronomers, scientists, and pilots, there was one report in particular that shook SIGN experts.

The incident took place on July 24, 1948. A DC-3 of Eastern Airlines took off from Houston, Texas, and headed toward Atlanta,

---

[5] Hesseman, pp. 39-40

[6] Hesseman, p. 40

Georgia. It was piloted by Clarence C. Chiles and John B. Whitted. Both were experienced flyers. At twenty miles southwest of Montgomery, Alabama, Capt. Chiles saw a light coming toward them at a speed unusual for a fighter plane or any other conventional aircraft. When the object was closer, Chiles saw that it was a huge, wingless aircraft, twice the diameter of a B-29 with no protruding surfaces. The cabin resembled a large cockpit and a blue light radiated from the sides of the object. The pilot stated that this object had come so close to his plane that he had to turn the aircraft to avoid a midair collision. After a few seconds, it seemed as if the UFO was alerted to the presence of the airliner, and with a large burst of flame from its after burners, the object disappeared into the cloud at an unusual speed. The jet wash from the after burner of the UFO left the plane rocking for a few seconds. Minutes after the incident, the object was seen over Robins Air Force Base in Georgia. The Air Technical Intelligence Center (ATIC) had received one more sighting report that night from a pilot flying between the border of West Virginia and North Carolina. He reported seeing a bright star shooting in the direction of Montgomery.

The ATIC report caused a greater stir than the Mantell incident. This was the first time that two reliable sources had seen a UFO from such a close proximity, and had returned home to tell about it. The description of windows in the UFO seemed to confirm the idea that the UFO was manned. ATIC, still skeptical of the reports of the pilots, started questioning the passengers that were on board. The incident had taken place at 2:45 a.m. and all passengers were asleep except one. He too reported seeing a glowing object. His description seemed to match that given by the two pilots. After this incident, the supporters of the "space visitor's theory" in the Defense Department felt more confident in their belief.[7]

On September 5, 1948, a report classified as "top secret" was forwarded to the ATIC as an "evaluation of the situation." It concluded that UFOs were of interplanetary origin.[8] After a thorough analysis, it seemed clear that no other possibility existed. When the report ended up in the hands of Chief of Staff Gen. Hoyt S. Vandenberg, he rejected the conclusion. Experts involved in Project SIGN visited the Pentagon for a detailed discussion, but Gen. Vandenberg remained unconvinced of their concluding opinion. Thus, in February 1949, Project SIGN's contract ended. The final concluding report, which was sent under a code number of F-TR-2274-1-A, was classified as secret. The report contained various possibilities explaining the nature of UFOs. In spite of the negative attitude from Washington and the Pentagon, the possibility of interplanetary spacecrafts was forwarded and carefully "sandwiched" between other explanations. It read as follows:

3. Spaceships: The following considerations pertain:
a. If there is an extraterrestrial civilization that can make such objects as are reported, then it is most probable that its development is far in advance of ours. This argument can be supported on probability arguments alone without recourse to astronomical hypothesis.
b. Such a civilization might observe that on earth we might now have atomic bombs and are fast developing rockets. In view of the past history of

---

[7] Hesseman, pp. 40-42
[8] Hesseman, p. 42

mankind, they should be alarmed. We should, therefore, expect such visits at this time and be prepared for them.

c.   Since the acts of mankind most easily observed from a distance are A-bomb explosions, we should expect some correlation between A-Bomb explosions, the time at which the spaceships are seen, and the time required for such spaceships to arrive from and return to home base.[9]

Project GRUDGE

After February 1949, top scientists from Project SIGN were replaced and investigations continued under a different name: Project GRUDGE! It is believed that those in the Pentagon, who were not convinced that UFOs were of extraterrestrial origin or constituted a threat to the United States, started seeing UFO investigations as a nuisance. It can be easily noticed that the name of the project, "GRUDGE" was, in fact, a reflection of the government's attitude toward UFO investigations. This new project tended mostly to confine its study to the reports of air force officers where the sightings occurred. Civilian experts and scientists under air force contract were kept away from the project. Right from the beginning, the main objective of GRUDGE was to prove that UFOs are not real; the Pentagon would now confine itself to those individuals that would confirm that.[10]

On May 11, 1950, a mysterious flying object appeared in the skies of McMinville, Oregon. Farmer Paul Trent and his wife noticed the silvery flash in the sky. Later, it turned out to be a big, disc-shaped

---

[9] Hesseman, p. 45 (published in Secret History)
[10] Hesseman, p. 49

object that was silver in color with a glint of bronze. Paul Trent brought the camera from his house and took two quick snaps of the UFO. The couple reported feeling a slight gust of wind as the object went by them. In a few seconds, it had disappeared. When the photographs were developed, they showed very clearly a disc-shaped saucer exactly the way it had been described by Mr. and Mrs. Trent.[11] A few days later, the Trents called journalist William Powell who at once came and took the accounts of the couple and the photographs. When they were analyzed by the newspaper's photo laboratory, nothing came out that would classify the photographs as fake. After the photo's publication on June 8, 1950, many other witnesses came out stating that they too had seen the object in the same vicinity. Within a few days, the FBI appeared to ask the couple for more information. The office of the newspaper was raided by the air force and the photographic prints were confiscated. After analysis, the air force concluded that the pictures did show an object that could not be conventionally explained. Twenty-eight years later, in 1958, the University of Colorado evaluated these photographic prints and came to the conclusion that the photographs were genuine.[12]

By the end of December 30, 1949, Project GRUDGE released its closing report. It was concluded that all reports of UFOs could be traced back to conventional aircrafts, mass hysteria, "war nerves," hoaxes, publicity stunts, and mentally deranged people. With this, Col. Harold E. Watson, explaining the position of the U.S. Air Force on UFOs, announced that "behind almost every report analyzed was

---

[11] Hesseman, p. 50

[12] Hesseman, pp. 50-54

a crack pot, a cultist, a publicity hound, or a joker."[13] To many who were following the developments, the statement and the conclusion of project GRUDGE came as a shock, for there was photographic evidence that could not be ruled out as "fake," and it could not have been a result of mass hysteria or the imagination of a delusional person. Furthermore, three days later, a spokesman for the U.S. Air Force Intelligence, Major Jeremiah Boggs, stated at a press conference, "The air force is intent on getting hold of a UFO for studying, and has therefore instructed its pilot to bring one of them in, using all means available, even if they have to catch it by the tail." The statement was made in the presence of Gen. S. Smith, the Chief of the USAF Public Information Office.

On August 25, 1951, an incident occurred that gave the press a solid case to challenge the results of Project GRUDGE. Four university professors saw an aerial phenomenon that they described as a squadron of round lights that flew over them at a very fast speed. These professors were Dr. W. I. Robinson (Geology), Dr. A. G. Oberg (Chemistry), Professor W. L Ducker (Petroleum Engineering), and Dr. George (Physics). The total number of the lights was counted thirty. Minutes later, the phenomenon repeated itself, and this time the professors were able to see that the objects radiated a bluish light. While witnesses of most sightings were generally ruled out by Project GRUDGE as publicity seekers or mentally delusional people, the witnesses of this particular sighting were more than credible. They were all senior academics and professors at Texas Technolog-

---

[13] Hesseman, p. 14

ical College in Lubbock. Five days later, a twenty-five-year-old student succeeded in photographing two separate formations of flying objects that flew over his house. The photographs seemed to confirm the description of the UFOs given earlier by the university professors.[14]

With these incidents, the press began to challenge the results of GRUDGE and the air force soon had to modify its stance. A secret meeting of general staff was held at the Pentagon and a joint instruction was dispatched as Joint Army, Navy, Air Force Publication (JANAP). Officially known as Communication Instruction for Reporting Vital Intelligence Sightings (CIRVIS), this was sent to all three armed forces. The word UFO was clearly mentioned in the document[15] and the document further stated that the contents of the report were protected by the Communications Act of 1934 and its amendments. It further stated that the document contained information affecting the national defense of the United States within the ambit of espionage laws. This means that the document's secrecy was classified at a level where transmitting any unauthorized information regarding its content was to be treated as espionage, for which the penalty was a fine of $10,000 and/or imprisonment of up to ten years. Once again, air force planes were fitted with cameras to film UFOs, and the pilots were given sealed envelopes that were only to be opened in case of a UFO sighting.

---

[14] Hesseman, pp. 54 - 55

[15] Hesseman, p. 54

Thus GRUDGE began its work again on October 27, 1951, and this time it was called Project Blue Book.[16]

UFOs Filmed by Naval Intelligence

In April 1952, a UFO sighting occurred and this time the witness was the topmost U.S. official, Naval Secretary Dan A. Kimball. While flying to Honolulu, Hawaii, two disc-shaped bodies approached his aircraft at an extremely fast speed and were seen by crew officers and reporters on the flight. "Their speed was incredible," Secretary Kimball stated later in an interview with Donald Keyhoe. "My pilots estimated it to be at over 2000 miles per hour! The two objects circled around us before shooting eastwards. At about fifty miles behind us there was another naval aircraft with Admiral Arthur Redford on board. I told my pilot to inform them about our sighting. A couple of seconds later, Redford's pilots called us to say the objects were circling around their airplane. A few seconds later, he called again to say they were out of sight. They must have covered the fifty miles in less than two seconds."[17]

After landing at Honolulu, Secretary Kimball radioed the air force and asked them what they intended to do about the presence of UFOs in U.S. airspace. He was told that it was against air force regulations to discuss sightings with the witness. Kimball called Rear Admiral Calvin Bolster, Chief of Office of Naval Research and

---

[16] Hesseman p. 56
[17] Hesseman, p. 64

ordered him to carry out the navy's own investigations of unexplained aerial phenomenon, independent of the air force.[18]

Two months later, the navy had a case, which was documented on film. Naval officer Delbert C. Newhouse, who was serving as a photographic reporter, turned in a two hundred-foot-long filmstrip that he had made of mysterious flying objects over Utah on Highway 30. The objects were filmed in a manner that would later help evaluate the speed of the object. The camera would be focused at a point so as to let the objects fly across the field of vision.

The footage was sent to the Naval Photographic Laboratory in Anacosta and was analyzed for three months. After six hundred working-hours of analysis, it was pointed out that with the lenses used, conventional aircrafts would have been identifiable at a distance of five miles. At that distance, their speed would have been 625 mph. No squadron of aircrafts was capable of flying in formation and carrying out such maneuvers at that speed. The possibility of balloons and birds was also ruled out because of the speed factor. After taking into consideration other factors, such as light reflection and angle of movement, the final conclusion of the experts was "unidentified objects under intelligent control."[19] Project Blue Book carried out a second analysis and it led to the same result. This caused a big stir at the Pentagon and on July 24, 1952, President Harry S. Truman and Chief of Staff Gen. Omar N. Bradley gave orders to shoot down all UFOs[20] that disobeyed the instruction to land. This

---

[18] Hesseman, p. 64

[19] Hesseman, p. 65

[20] Hesseman, p. 69

was the first time in the history of the United States that such an order was given.

The following month, in August of 1952, the final report for Project Blue Book was written. Of the 1,593 cases that Project Blue Book investigated, 18.51 percent were identified as balloons, 11.66 percent as airplanes, 14.2 percent as astronomical (i.e., planets and meteorites, etc.), 1.66 percent as hoaxes, 22.72 percent as those with insufficient data, and 26.94 percent as unidentified flying objects.[21]

The Plane That Was Swallowed by a UFO

One year after the final report of Project Blue Book, an incident occurred at Kinross Airbase at Lake Michigan that resulted in the disappearance of an F-89 fighter and its pilot. A radar officer detected an unidentified object over the security zone of the airbase on November 23, 1953. The object was performing strange maneuvers. The commander of the airbase checked with the headquarters to find out if any planes were operating in the area, but the answer was negative. When various attempts to establish radio contact with the flier failed, pilot Felix Moncla was ordered to fly toward the UFO and identify the object at close range. At 9:18 p.m., Lt. Felix Moncla and his radar officer Lt. R. R. Wilson started their F-89 fighter. The cloudy weather prevented the pilot from getting a clear visual, but he pursued the object. For nine minutes, ground control watched the chase closely on the radar screens. It had become obvious that an

---

[21] Hesseman, p. 75

engagement was taking place in the air, and the commander was just about to give the order to fire when both radar blips collided and became one. The ground kept on calling Moncla on the radio but there was no response. The blip took off at a terrific speed and disappeared from the radar screen.

The only logical explanation was a midair collision. It was understood by the ground station that the plane had collided with the UFO, had crashed, and the UFO was still in a condition to fly away. The search for the wreckage went on for days and involved not just airplanes and helicopters, but boats of American as well as Canadian coast guards. Every inch of territory where the plane could have possibly crashed was scanned, but nothing could be found. Not a single piece of wreckage was discovered. There was no trace of a crash. The F-89 had disappeared from the sky along with the two officers. The official explanation given by the air force stated that the plane had crashed while pursuing an aircraft of the Canadian Air Force. The Canadian government denied the incident and pointed out that at that time the Royal Canadian Air Force did not have an aircraft over the Great Lakes Area.[22]

General MacArthur on UFOs

On October 6, 1955, legendary general of the Second World War, Gen. Douglas MacArthur made a statement that shook the world. "I believe that owing to the advances in science, the nations of the earth should unite in order to survive and present a common front

---

[22] Hesseman, pp. 77-79

against attacks by people from other planets," the four-star general stated during his visit to Naples. In May of 1962, he again spoke about a war in which humanity would be united against alien powers from another planet.[23] Much later it became known that Gen. Douglas MacArthur had created a research team called the Interplanetary Phenomenon Unit (IPU) to investigate unexplained aerial phenomenon. This unit functioned from the end of Second World War until 1954. What exactly did the IPU discover that made the general make such remarks is not known. The files of this unit are held in strict secrecy even today; although its existence was confirmed long ago.[24]

The Jimmy Carter Incident

On September 18, 1973, while he was still a governor, former U.S. President Jimmy Carter filled out a UFO sighting report form for the National Investigation Committee on Aerial Phenomenon (NICAP). This form contained information regarding Carter's own sighting in October 1969. He had arrived for his speech at the Lions Club in Leary, Georgia, and was being greeted by the reception committee, when they all saw a bright light in the sky flying toward them. When the light came to a distance of five hundred yards, the group noticed that its color changed rapidly, going through a whole spectrum from violet to red. According to the form that Carter filed four years later, the sighting had lasted ten to twelve minutes. It is also known that after this sighting and before running for the presidency in 1976,

---

[23] Hesseman, p. 48

[24] Hesseman, p. 48

Carter had said that if he became president, he would "make every piece of information this country has about UFO sightings available to the public and the scientists."[25] While he could not release "every" piece of information to the American people, he kept his word as much as he could. Around 20,000 pages of top-secret documents, which until that time had been kept secret, were released under his presidency. Most of the information in this chapter comes from those documents.

Majestic 12

Majestic 12 is beyond a doubt the single most significant UFO-related document to come out of the U.S. government's classified files. It is still a mystery as to how a document as secret as Majestic 12 could possibly leak out.

On December 11, 1984, Jamie Shandera, a Hollywood film producer, opened his mailbox and found a large, brown envelope. It had no sender's address. The stamp had a postmark from Albuquerque, New Mexico. Inside the large envelope was another envelope sealed with plastic tape. Shandera was surprised to find a third envelope; it was white with the emblem of the Marriott hotel and inside he found undeveloped 35mm Kodak film. When the reel came back from the photo lab, only eight frames had been exposed. They showed pictures of what appeared to be a highly classified government document bearing a "TOP SECRET/MAJIC EYES ONLY" stamp. The document had been put under a secrecy level so high

---

[25] Hesseman, pp. 302-303

that only those holding a special access permit designated "MAJIC" were authorized to view it. Its "EYES ONLY" classification means that the document was meant for reading only. The reader could not make photocopies of it nor make any notes from it.

The document, dated November 18, 1952, was a briefing paper addressed to President Dwight D. Eisenhower. It was meant to inform him, before he was sworn in as the president, about the status of a top secret UFO project that the United States government had been carrying out since 1947. The document revealed that while SIGN, GRUDGE, and Blue Book were being carried out, the United States Air Force was already in possession of an alien spacecraft that had crashed in Roswell, New Mexico. These papers went on to say that not only did the United States Air Force have wreckage from the crash, but also had in its possession five alien bodies. The report was made by the first Director of the CIA, Adm. Roscoe H. Hillenkoeter and was signed by former U.S. President Harry Truman.[26]

It is known today that on July 6, 1947, the 509th Bomb Group, the only atom bomb unit in the United States Air Force, was called to investigate a "crash" in Roswell, New Mexico.[27] Major Jesse Marcell of the Intelligence Corps and Sheridan Cavitt of the Counter Espionage Unit were sent to investigate the wreckage of an "unidentified flying object." The air force base issued a statement to the press the next day announcing: "The many rumors regarding the flying disc became a reality yesterday when the intelligence office of 509th Bomb Group

---

[26] Hesseman, pp. 337-339
[27] Hesseman, p. 340

of the 8th Air Force in Roswell was fortunate enough to gain possession of a disc through the cooperation of the local ranchers and the sheriff's office of Chaves County. The flying object landed on a ranch near Roswell sometime last week . . . action was immediately taken, and the disc was picked up at the rancher's home."[28]

When this statement was issued, the air force believed that the "flying saucer" they had recovered was a crashed spy plane. But soon the main portion of the wreckage was picked up by aerial surveillance, and also found with the craft were five alien bodies.[29] It thus became clear that what they had discovered was an extraterrestrial spacecraft and not a spy plane. Immediately, a large-scale retrieval operation was initiated. The military cordoned off all roads leading to the ranchland northwest of Roswell until every piece of debris had been recovered. Servicemen scanned every inch of territory in order to pick up anything suspicious—anything that could be even remotely connected to the "crash." Meanwhile, the press release issued earlier regarding the recovery of a flying disc was retrieved the same day, and another press conference was called in which Gen. Roger M. Ramey at the Fort Worth Air Base declared to the journalists that the flying disc was, in fact, a crashed weather balloon. Fragments of one such balloon were displayed for journalists to take pictures.

The Majestic12 document goes on to reveal that after the recovery the best scientists in the country were called together to

[28] Hesseman, pp. 341-342
[29] Hesseman, p. 346

analyze the findings. They were to conduct their research under scientist Dr. Vannevar Bush. On September 19, 1947, a status report that was sent to President Truman stated that the research team had concluded that the crashed vessel was a short-range reconnaissance craft of nonterrestrial origin. On September 24, 1947, Dr. Vannevar Bush and Defense Secretary Forrestal were called to a meeting in the White House. The meeting that took place in the Oval Office between the president, Dr. Bush, and secretary Forrestal is not only mentioned in the Majestic 12 document, but is also in the records of President Truman that are archived in the Truman Library. It was during this meeting that the establishment of Majestic 12 was decided. The team was to consist of top-brass military and the scientific minds of the time. Besides Bush and Forrestal, the other ten members of the Majestic 12 team were:

- Vice Admiral Roscoe H. Hillenkoetter, commander of the Intelligence Corps in the Pacific Theatre during World War II. He was also the first director of the CIA.
- General Hoyt S. Vandenberg, Chief of Staff of the U.S. Air Force and former director of the CIA.
- Dr. Detlev Bronk, chairman of the National Research Council and member of the Medical Advisory Board of the Atomic Energy Commission.
- Dr. Jerome Hunsaker, an aircraft designer from the Massachusetts Institute of Technology and chair of the National Advisory Committee for Aeronautics.
- Rear Admiral Sidney M. Sauers, former director of the CIA and then executive secretary of the U.S. National Security Council.

- Gordon Gray, assistant secretary and later Secretary of the Unites States Army.

- Dr. Donald Menzel, director of the observatory of Howard University who had worked on secret projects with the National Security Agency (NSA).

- General Robert M. Montague, commander of the Atomic Commission installation at the Sandia Base, Albuquerque, New Mexico, weapons testing grounds.

- Dr. Lloyd V. Berkner, executive secretary of the Research and Development Board. He was a cofounder for the development and evaluation group for weapon systems.

- General Nathan F. Twining, Commander of Technical Intelligence of the Air Force (then AMC and later ATIC). It is known that he had cancelled his planned journey to the west coast and flew to New Mexico to supervise the action at Roswell.

The team was to proceed with all due speed and caution and was to refer to the matter only as Operation Majestic 12.[30]

The first foreigner to know about the existence of MJ-12 was Canadian Wilbert B. Smith. On November 21, 1950, Controller of Telecommunications at the Canadian Department of Transport received a memo from Smith in which he talked about a top-secret U.S. project classified under a level of secrecy even higher than the H-bomb.[31] He had acquired this information from Robert I.

---

[30] Hesseman, p. 345

[31] Hesseman, p. 347

Sarbacher, a scientist at the Pentagon. Sarbacher also revealed that his colleagues believed that the alien bodies recovered were biological robots. The Pentagon referred to these as Extraterrestrial Biological Entities (EBEs). It is believed that they are still in the possession of the U.S. military and, according to some UFO researchers, they are kept in AREA-51—the most secret military facility in the United States.

CHAPTER 2

CLOSE ENCOUNTERS OF THE FOURTH KIND

Modern Cases of Alien Contact

His name was Professor Allen J. Hynek and he was the professor of astronomy at Northwestern University. In 1948, he was recruited by the U.S. Air Force to carry out research into the UFO phenomenon. As an advisor to the air force on UFOs, he served as the scientific consultant on three major UFO investigations: Project SIGN, Project GRUDGE, and Project Blue Book. Far from conclusively dismissing the subject, Hynek became convinced that the UFO phenomenon was a real mystery to be studied. For an accurate analysis of UFO reports, he devised a classification system that was based on the distance from the observer and that divided the reports in to two broad categories—Distant Encounters (in which UFOs were spotted from a distance greater than 150 meters) and Close Encounters (in which they were spotted from less than 150 meters.)

Distant Encounters were further divided into three categories: Nocturnal Lights (UFOs were seen as lights in the night sky); Daylight Discs (there was enough daylight to make out the disc shape of the UFO); and Radar Visuals (UFOs were also spotted by military radars). Close Encounters were also divided into three main categories: Close Encounters of the First Kind were simply eye-witness reports in which the witness claimed to be less than 150 meters away from the UFO); Close Encounters of the Second Kind were cases in which the presence of the UFO had caused a physical effect on the environment. For example, in some instances the area in which the UFO supposedly landed showed landing marks or radiation burns on the ground. These were cases with a greater degree of credibility; "UFOologists" had something more "concrete" to analyze than a mere eyewitness account. Close Encounters of the Third Kind were cases in which the occupants of UFOs were also seen. This system has been used since then by UFO researchers around the world to compile and classify reports of unexplained aerial phenomenon.

Later on, when more research was completed on the UFO phe-nomenon, researchers were coming across cases that could not be classified into Hynek's classification system. These cases were so bizarre and so unbelievable that they came to be known as "Close Encounters of the Fourth Kind." This is a chapter about them.

The Missing Time

It was September 19, 1961. The time was 11 p.m. Barney Hill, a postal employee, and his wife Betty, a forty-one-year-old social worker, were returning from Niagara Falls after a short vacation. As the car drove through the White Mountains, the couple noticed a light in the sky that began to follow them. Near North Woodstock,

Barney got out with a pair of binoculars to investigate the "light."
As he examined the object through the binoculars, he noticed that
the light was a "pancake"-shaped disc that was coming toward them.
He had never seen an object like that before. Obviously frightened,
Barney returned to the car and drove off with the light still following
them. When they were passing near Indian Head, the couple heard
loud beeping sounds, which made their vehicle vibrate for a while.
Then the car went through an invisible barrier and when it came
out on the other end, the scenery was different. The couple was
driving thirty-five miles down from the spot where they had entered
the invisible barrier.

They were both confused. When they finally arrived home, they
thought it was 3:00 a.m. Instead, they were stunned beyond belief to
find that it was 5:00 a.m. The invisible barrier through which the
couple passed had somehow distorted the time and space. They both
felt very confused and disoriented. Barney felt a strange soreness in
his genitals, which he examined in front of the mirror. In the days
after that, Betty began having nightmares. In her sleep, she would
see strange people with gray skins, big noses, and dark hair. These
men would insert needles into her stomach and perform various
painful medical procedures. Betty was convinced that these dreams
were caused by something that happened when they went through
the invisible barrier.

On September 26, Betty wrote a letter to NICAP (National
Investigation Committee on Aerial Phenomenon) in which she
stated that she was seeking psychiatric help. A retired officer of the
U.S. Marines and a world-renowned UFO researcher, Major Donald
Keyhoe, headed NICAP at the time. On October 21, he sent an

astronomer Walter Webb, on behalf of NICAP to investigate the case. After interrogating the couple for six hours, Webb concluded that both individuals were credible and that they had undergone a simultaneous amnesia—a "memory lapse" which was calculated to be of two hours duration.

In March of 1962, Barney's groin soreness turned into warts, which had to be surgically removed. Now, there was concrete medical evidence that Barney was exposed to something during the time distortion, which caused the warts. Barney's doctor, Patrick Quirke, sympathetically listened to the story and became convinced that the couple had undergone an extremely unusual experience that night. The case was far beyond what medical science could explain. Thus, the Hills' ended up with Dr. Benjamin Simon, a leading Boston psychiatrist.

Dr. Simon was a UFO skeptic who refused to believe that there was any "paranormal" reality to the Hills' case. He was, however, convinced that the Hills' case was genuine and that there was a period of two hours that was missing from their memories. They were suffering from a "shared amnesia" not known to medical science before then. In order to solve the mystery, Dr. Simon decided to give the patients hypnotic regression. The procedure involved putting the two subjects in a hypnotic trance and taking them back to that time period when they were driving through White Mountain. Under hypnosis, the subjects were able to recall in great detail what happened to them during the night of September 19, 1961. The hypnosis session showed that the "nightmares" that Betty was having about strange beings performing experiments were not just dreams. They did happen!

They were driving home that night when the light in the sky began following them. Barney got out of the car with a pair of binoculars to examine the object. When the object came after him, he got into their vehicle and drove off. They had not gotten very far when the close proximity of the UFO began to cause vibrations in the car. The UFO landed on the road and Barney recalled how people who were not human took them into the spacecraft. The couple was then separated and medical tests were performed on them. Barney had sperm samples taken, while Betty experienced a needle placed into her abdomen. After completion of these tests, memory of this two-hour-long incident was deleted from their minds and they were placed thirty-five miles away from where they had been taken. It was this that made the 120-minute episode seem like a split-second time and space distortion.

The case finally made it in the news in 1965 through a local Boston newspaper. Later, the couple and their doctors agreed to talk to local columnist John Fuller who promised to write a book about them. *The Interrupted Journey* by John Fuller was published in 1966. The book, when it came out, captured people's fascination in such a way that it launched a wave of alien abduction stories. Eight years after the abduction, Barney Hill developed a brain hemorrhage and passed away.[32]

Barney and Betty Hill's case was interesting, but it wasn't the only one of its kind. In 1981, Budd Hopkins, a New York artist, wrote a book titled *The Missing Time* in which he documented a series of

---

[32] Randles, pp. 29-32

abduction cases from all across the United States. Hopkins' research showed that unrelated witnesses, who had never known each other, were giving accounts that were remarkably similar.

In most cases, individuals who underwent abduction experienced a few minutes or a few hours that were missing from their lives. For example, in a typical abduction, a woman gets up in the morning to make breakfast. She checks the clock on the wall and finds the time to be 7:00 a.m. She takes an egg out of the fridge and breaks it on a frying pan. The next minute she finds the kitchen full of smoke and the fried egg has been burnt beyond recognition. She opens the windows to let the smoke out, and switches on the exhaust fan. How could the egg burn in one second? There is no logical answer. She is totally confused. She looks at the clock and the time is 7:45 a.m. At that moment, she realizes that the egg had been on the pan for forty-five minutes. That one second in her experience was forty-five minutes in real time!

If you have undergone such a time distortion, then there is a possibility that you could be one of those individuals who have undergone what UFO investigators describe as Close Encounters of the Fourth Kind. Under hypnosis, these people reveal that during that missing time they witnessed a "flying saucer" or a UFO in the sky whose presence interfered with electronic instruments nearby—a television would lose its image; the engine of the car would not start, etc. Furthermore, they recall being taken into the spacecraft by humanoid beings that were not exactly human. In most cases, these beings would flash a paralyzing stun-beam on the individual that would cause the person to "freeze" in his place. Then he/she would be taken into a spacecraft, where medical procedures would be performed on him/her. The medical tests people describe under hypnosis can vary from a simple collection of saliva samples, to advanced surgeries with needles being inserted into the subject's belly. Procedures dealing with the human reproductive system are the ones most commonly reported. In men, the aliens would take sperm samples (as described by Barney Hill), and in women they would take vaginal fluid or place a needle through the stomach. Some subjects also describe skin and tissue being taken from different parts of the body.

After these medical tests are completed, the subject is put back in the same spot from where he or she was taken, and all memory of the incident is deleted in such a manner that the whole length of time appears to be a split-second time distortion. Later on, these individuals will find scars or surgical marks on their bodies, but will not recall how they got them. They will feel afraid, but will not know the cause of their fear. They will feel extremely depressed, but will not know the cause of their depression. This disturbed state of their mind can be traced back to those few hours that are missing from their lives. After the Hills' case in 1961, the second abduction to be studied under hypnosis was in 1962. This time the location was Stendal, East Germany.

Stendal, East Germany (Former Communist German Democratic Republic), January 1962

It was a cold January evening in Stendal, the Former Communist Republic of Germany. The time was around 6:30 p.m. Eighteen-year-old Norbert Haase and his friends were having fun skating on a frozen lake when Norbert noticed something in the sky. He pointed it out to his friends, but they did not pay much attention. When the play was over and the boys were going home, Norbert's brother insisted that he should come with them, but Norbert stayed on the lake looking up into the sky. Something held him back. Soon, the boys were out of sight and Norbert was left alone in the field gazing at the sky.

On the far side of the lake, there was a little island that used to be a haven for ducks and swans. All of a sudden, Norbert wanted to go there. So, he started walking toward it. He was only fifty yards from the island when a bright light lit up behind the island and shot up. It was as if someone had suddenly switched it on. It was bright and radiant, bluish-white in color, beautiful, but at the same time frightening. It was nothing Norbert had seen before. He stood there stunned and fascinated. Soon, he was blinded by the extreme brightness of the light as the disc hovered fifteen feet above the ground. In the next moment, Norbert found himself five hundred feet away from the island. He had a terrible headache and his eyes hurt. His skates were lying near him. Shocked and confused, he stood up not knowing how he had traveled so far away from the lake in a split second. He looked at his watch, but it had stopped at 6:40 p.m.

Norbert's parents lived in a small railway colony close to the lake. When he arrived home, he found his mother greatly worried about him. When she saw her son, she was shocked! His skin was tanned to a bright shade of pink as if he had been exposed to extreme sunlight. That was not possible, because there was no bright sun at that time. On the right side of his nose he had a small wound from where a layer of his skin had been removed. It was obvious something had happened to him on the lake. He had been exposed to an extremely powerful light source, and a skin sample had been taken from his face. The next day, Norbert's father took him to a physician, Dr. Boos, who had treated Norbert since childhood. Upon failing to make any diagnoses, Dr. Boos sent Norbert to the polyclinic at Stendal. During the next two nights, Norbert had disturbed sleep. He kept talking in his sleep and would wake up in the middle of the night bathed in sweat. He was told later that, in his sleep, he talked about God, space, and time. Upon waking, when he was told he had been talking in his sleep about God and astronomy, he found it hard to believe because he had never thought of these things.

Two days later, two STASI officers (Secret Service of East Germany) visited Norbert while he was still at the polyclinic. They made him fill out a questionnaire, which read "Unidentified and Other Kinds of Phenomenon." They asked him a lot of questions—one of which was whether or not he knew what an "UFO" was. He replied in the negative because in those days, the word "UFO" was unknown in the Communist German Democratic Republic. Six days after the incident, two psychologists from Leipzig came to see him at the clinic. They wanted to put him under hypnosis and make him remember what had happened to him that night. Norbert agreed to the procedure.

Over the next three days, he was hypnotized and questioned for two to three hours. Eight audiotapes were made of Norbert recalling the incident under hypnosis. To their question of where he was, he had answered that he was lying on an operating table. When asked if there were other people around, he had described beautiful, slim people with white overalls. On their attire, he remembered seeing a symbol; it was the tree of life from mythology, but without the snake. The snake was present on the collar instead.

The contact changed Norbert's life. He became more withdrawn and started thinking about God, life, and the universe. In 1968, he was serving in the National People's Army when he was sent to the Czechoslovakian Socialist Republic. During the People's Revolution in Prague, he disobeyed the orders to shoot at people and had to spend four years in a military prison. In 1974, he was finally extradited to the Federal Republic of Germany.[33]

Ashland, Nebraska, December 3, 1967

It is often reported that the presence of a UFO causes agitation in animals. Dogs would start barking or cattle would act excited. At 1:30 a.m. in Ashland, Nebraska, the stalls of cattle at the local cattle market started mooing in panic. When local police officer, Herbert Schirmer, visited the cattle stalls, he found no apparent reason for their excitement. Yet, they went around their stalls trampling their hooves.

Later, at 2:30 a.m. while he was driving back from the cattle farm, he noticed blinking red lights at the end of the road. Thinking that it was a broken down truck, Officer Schirmer switched on the headlights of his police car as he drove toward it. Suddenly, he stopped; he was in shock. What he was expecting to be a truck was a polished-silver, oval-shaped object hovering about six feet above the ground. Officer Schirmer later described its shape like that of an American football. It was not a helicopter, for it had no rotors, and

---

[33] Hesseman, pp. 427-429

it was not a plane for it had no wings. It was just an aluminum-colored, oval shape that floated in the air. While he was still trying to make out all the details, a bright orange flame shot out from beneath the object and shot upward and disappeared into the night sky. He grabbed his log book and noted the time (2:30 a.m.) and sighting of the mysterious object.

In the next five minutes, he was back at the police station. To his amazement, the clock showed 3:00 a.m. He had seen the object at 2:30 a.m. and it would have taken him less than ten minutes to get to the police station, but for some reason it was thirty minutes later. There was a period of twenty minutes that was unaccounted for on his drive back to the station. In addition to that, he felt dizzy and weak. He stayed in the office for over an hour, and then returned home that morning at 5:00 a.m. While undressing, he noticed a scar on his leg, but could not remember how he had gotten it.

The police department informed the air force the next morning and Schirmer was given the orders to contact the Colorado study group. A few days later, Schirmer found himself being interrogated by physicist professor, Roy Craig; psychologist professor, Roy Sprinkle from the University of Wyoming; and Sprinkle's assistant John Ashland. In addition to questioning Schirmer, the three investigators also spoke to his colleagues at work, his neighbors, and his family. After a thorough investigation, they were convinced that the subject was a credible witness. Still Schirmer went through a lie detector test, which he passed without difficulty. It was clear that he had seen something that night and that there were twenty lost minutes of which he had no memory.

In order to recover the lost memory of the missing time, Professor Sprinkle suggested hypnotherapy. Officer Herbert Schirmer was then hypnotized and taken back to that time period when he had encountered the UFO. Under hypnosis, Schirmer began to recall the details of the missing time. He revealed that he was at the crossing of highway 6 and 63 when he saw the disc-shaped object. It generated some kind of magnetic force that literally dragged the car uphill toward the UFO. Soon, two figures came out of the landed craft and one of them paralyzed him with a green light. He remembered how he wanted to go for his handgun, but found himself paralyzed by the light. He was then taken inside the UFO where he saw, in the middle of the craft, something that looked like half a cocoon. It rotated and produced multicolored lights. Schirmer also had the memory of nonverbal communication that he had with the occupants of the UFO. He obviously had questions in his mind and the beings were able to "sense" these in his thoughts. They answered his questions through some form of telepathic communication. He was thinking, "Why are these things here?" And they told him that they were there to get electricity. They would get that from a high voltage tower connected directly to the Ashland powerhouse. After spending some time on board, he was taken out of the UFO back to his car. The being that left him near his car told him that he would not remember what he had seen or heard. He would only remember seeing something landing and taking off. It happened! The only conscious memory Officer Schirmer had was of seeing something land and then take off.

Investigations by the Colorado study group showed that Schirmer was a credible witness; he was an honest and reliable police officer with a good service record. He was definitely not a publicity seeker or someone suffering from hallucinations. Results from the lie detector test also confirmed the conclusion made by the Colorado study group, and then, of course, there was the account taken under hypnosis.[34] It is not possible for all three unrelated aspects of the investigation to come to the same conclusion. Something happened that night.

Bahia Blanca, Brazil, January 5, 1975

Carlos Diaz was a railway worker who also worked nights as a waiter in order to be able to raise his young son. It was 4:00 a.m. and, after finishing his night duty, he was walking the streets of Bahia Blanca when a bluish-white light blinded him. The next sensation he had was of floating in the air as if being carried away by an invisible force. He then lost consciousness.

His next memory was of awakening inside a closed room feeling dizzy and sick. A tall being appeared and performed medical tests on Diaz. At one point, Diaz extended a hand and touched this creature. Its texture felt like "rubber." The being then used a suction tube to extract tufts of hair. Once the procedure was complete, Diaz went through another blackout.

When he opened his eyes, he was lying on the side of a road. He looked at his watch and found that it had stopped at 3:50 a.m. The real time then was close to 8:00 a.m. Four hours had passed. As he was standing on the side of the road feeling confused, a passing motorist spotted him and, thinking that he had been hit by a car,

[34] Hesseman, pp. 156-159

offered to drive him to the nearest hotel. On his way to the hotel, he found out that he was not in Bahia Blanca, but in Retiro, three hundred miles away!

Back home in Bahia Blanca, Diaz's wife was worried sick as it had been hours and her husband had not returned from his night duty. She was totally stunned when the police called and told her that her husband was in Retiro. Totally confused as to how he ended up there, she got on the next train and traveled for eight hours to be by his bedside. The only thing Diaz remembered was the light that took him, the examination, and the hair removal. Doctors who examined him confirmed that hair was missing from its roots. The police found one more piece of startling evidence. Just before the abduction, Diaz had purchased a newspaper that was printed in Bahia Blanca. It was still with him. This was strange because at 8:00 a.m. it could not have been bought in Retiro because supplies took hours to get to that town.[35]

Apache-Sitgrea National Park, Arizona, November 5, 1975

Twenty-two-year-old Travis Walton was part of a seven-man lumberjack team that had finished work at 6:00 p.m. and was returning home. On their way, they saw a luminous disk vibrating and shining in an orange-yellow light. Travis broke from his group and approached the hovering disc to get a closer look. Suddenly, he was blinded by a flash of blue light and lost consciousness.

---

[35] Randles, p. 102

When he came back to his senses, he found himself lying at the edge of the road. He looked around and saw no sign of his friends. When he managed to get back on his feet, he realized that he was at a different location. When he staggered to the nearest gas station, he was shocked to find that he was near Herber, Arizona, thirty miles from where he fell unconscious. He was even more shocked to discover that the day was November 10. He had been gone for five days.

Soon, he found out that the police department had locked up his friends on suspicion of his murder. They had gone to the police station and reported that a ray of light coming from a "flying saucer" hit their friend. Police interrogated the six men, and their accounts seemed identical. They were even given a lie detector test, which they all cleared, except seventeen-year-old Steve Pierce who was far too terrified. This was the first time abduction had taken place in front of six witnesses.

Under hypnosis, Travis recalled lying on an operating table in a room with metal walls. He talked about strange people with large heads and big, dark eyes examining him. They looked like well-developed fetuses. He also had the memory of being taken into a large, clammy room where he saw a number of "flying saucers" similar to the one he had seen in the park. This indicated that he had been in some kind of a mothership that contained smaller UFOs similar to the one he had seen.

The Travis Walton case is treated as one of the best documented abduction cases today, but when it happened the incident did not receive the due attention. It got its public acclaim in the early 1990s when Paramount released the film *Fire in the Heavens: The True*

Story of Travis Walton. The film was produced by Tracy Torme, the producer of *Intruders*.[36]

Alamogordo, New Mexico, August 13, 1975

On August 13, 1975, a Close Encounter of the Fourth Kind (CE-4) occurred in New Mexico, and this time the victim was Charles L. Moody, a veteran of the Vietnam War who had served in the air force for fourteen years. That night, he had returned from Holloman Air Force Base after his night duty, and went out into the desert to watch a meteor shower. Local television had announced the ideal viewing time was 1:00 a.m. that night, so Moody waited patiently in his car under the desert sky. As an air force employee, Moody had been exposed to almost every type of aircraft, but what he saw that night was beyond his wildest imagination.

It was a large, metal disc around fifty-five feet wide, 18–20 feet high, and partly lit with multicolored lights. It descended from the sky and hovered above the ground only one hundred yards from him. After fluttering a bit, it stabilized itself and started coming toward the car. Moody wanted to drive away from the "thing," so he rolled up his window and tried to start the car but found the engine dead. With one eye on the approaching object, he tried again and again to start the car but the motor would not run. Now, the object was thirty feet away and Moody could hear a humming sound coming from it.

In the next second, he was sitting in the car dazed and watching the object disappear in the night sky. Then he turned on the ignition

---

[36] Hesseman, pp. 446-447

and the motor started running. He stepped on the gas and drove off. Upon arriving home, he went into the kitchen and looked at the wall clock. He could not believe his eyes. The time was 3:00 a.m. The last time he had checked his watch it was 1:15 a.m., and that was only minutes before the UFO appeared from the sky. He had undergone a time distortion. During the next few days, Moody experienced eruptions in his skin and pain in the lower part of his body. At the back of his mind, Moody somehow had the feeling that it was caused by the UFO he had seen in the desert. He contacted Dr. Abraham Goldman, a psychological and neurological counselor, and told him about his "experience." The doctor introduced him to self-hypnosis.

During the next few weeks, the lost memory of the missing hour returned to his conscious memory. The first thing he was able to recall was the humanoid beings with disproportionate physical features. Their heads were larger than a human's, their eyes and ears were small, and they had very thin lips. Then, he began to remember the details of the abduction. He recalled how he sat paralyzed in his car as two of these beings came towards him. The next thing he remembered was lying on a dull, metallic table that was like an operating table. It was placed in the middle of a dimly lit hall that did not have any visible source of lighting. The beings communicated to Moody in a non-verbal manner. They would read his thoughts and would communicate without speaking. They assured him in this "telepathic" conversation that there was no need to be afraid, and nothing would happen to him. Then Moody remembered other details about the interior of the vessel. He remembered going through a sliding door and standing in a room with thin pillars in the middle. They were going all the way through the ceiling. While he was watching the interior in amazement, he was "told" that this was not the main ship, but a small reconnaissance craft. The mothership was orbiting the earth somewhere between the altitudes of 400–6,000 miles. The last thing that he remembered was the alien putting both hands on Moody's head, and telling him that he was to forget everything he had seen. After a two-week period, he would gradually remember.

Moody's case was investigated by the Aerial Phenomenon Research Organization (APRO), the oldest UFO research organization in the United States. The organization specialized in investigating Close Encounters of the Third Kind. Before their investigation on Moody's case could be completed, Moody was transferred to Europe. APRO did not give up on Moody and pursued him all the way to Europe. There, he underwent a lie detector test and cleared it. APRO was convinced that Moody was a real contactee.[37]

Manhattan, New York, November 30, 1989

On November 30, 1989, an abduction took place in Manhattan, New York, (one of the most populated areas of the United States), and was witnessed by Manhattan residents nearby. The abductee, Linda Napolitano, was "taken" from her apartment in the middle of her sleep. She had been "floated" out of the window into a flying saucer that hovered near the apartment building, and then returned after the usual medical examination, probing, etc.

The case was investigated by world-renowned abduction investigator and the author of *The Missing Time*, Budd Hopkins. Hopkins

---

[37] Hesseman, pp. 451-453

was still on the case retrieving lost memories through hypnosis when he received a letter and a taped message from two security guards who had seen Linda being abducted.

The two security agents (identified as Dan and Richard) were performing a routine job and driving a world leader from his office to the nearby heliport, when all of a sudden the engine of their vehicle went dead and the headlights went out. There was little traffic on the streets because it was past 3:00 a.m. Dan grabbed his mobile radio and found it out of order. The telephone in the limousine was also dead. Fearing for the worst, the two agents got out of the car and, with his service revolver drawn, Dan scanned the nearby buildings for a possible ambush, while Richard pushed the car under an overpass.

In the next second, Dan was asking for binoculars; he had seen "something very strange" flying in the sky. The two men watched in silence and then one of them called, "Come out, sir! This you've gotta see!" The back door of the limo opened, and a man, no other than former UN Secretary General Xavier Perez de Cuellar, stepped down from his car to watch the scene.

It was a huge UFO that was two-thirds the width of the building. A beam of whitish-blue light came from it and focused on a window at the 12th floor. The three men watched alternately through the pair of binoculars as the scene unfolded before their eyes. The woman was described by the agents to be flying out of the window enveloped in a beam of light. She was wearing a white night dress and was curled in a fetal position. Along with her, they also saw three small beings with disproportionate heads, being "teleported" into the UFO. The disc then lit up and glided away at high speeds over the head of the three stunned men who had watched the scene.

When the men returned to their car, everything was functioning. They wanted to drive the Secretary General to the helipad but Perez refused to go. Instead, he ordered the men to stay on the side of the road because he wanted to see the thing again when it returned. They waited there for a while but the thing did not return. The motorcade then took off.

Xavier Perez de Cuellar denied any knowledge of the incident.[38] But the fact remained that Linda Napolitano had been abducted, and these security guards could not have known the time and the place unless they were present. The case was still under investigation when more witnesses turned up. Some people had witnessed exactly the same incident from over the bridge crossing the East River. The details that they were giving were similar to what the security guards had given. This became one of the most heavily scrutinized and most argued cases in abduction study, because it involved multiple witnesses that did not know each other (i.e., security guards and people on the bridge).

Victoria, Australia, 1994

This incident that occurred in the foothills of the Dandenong Mountains in Australia is often described as the most "perfect" abduction ever recorded. It has silenced some of the most hard-line skeptics.

It was past midnight on August 8, 1993. Kelly Cahill, a married mother of three, was returning from a friend's place along with her husband. Passing near Belgrave South, they drove toward a glowing,

---

[38] Hesseman, pp. 430-431

orange object hovering just above the treetops on the road ahead. It was described by Kelly to be round with glassy transparent patches or windows. Through these, the couple could make out human-like figures. Suddenly, the object disappeared from their view and moments later they were driving into an orange light.

When they came out through the other end, Kelly could smell vomit. She started feeling sick and settled back on her seat. Andrew, Kelly's husband, thought that they must have turned a corner or something because the UFO that they had seen in the sky was no longer there.

When they reached home, the couple was surprised to find that the time was 2:30 a.m. The journey seemed to have taken an hour more than it should have. Andrew suggested that they must have left their friend's home later than assumed. But their friend confirmed the departure time and it became apparent that an hour was "lost" on the road. While undressing, Kelly noticed a triangular cut or a scar just below her navel, and had no memory of how she got it. Kelly knew she was unwell because, right after the sighting, her period came days before its usual time. In less than a month, she was in the hospital being treated for womb infection. Kelly's case left doctors totally mystified because the only logical reason was a terminated pregnancy.

Almost two months later while driving down the same road, Kelly suddenly had a flashback in which she remembered what had happened during the lost hour. That night, the couple had seen a landed UFO beside the road. They stopped and got out of their cars to see tall, dark figures with large, red eyes "gliding" toward them. They had spoken telepathically saying that they meant no harm.

Then, Kelly recalled being thrown onto her back by an invisible force. She also had a recollection of another car that had stopped on the road. The same beings in dark suits had surrounded the passengers of the other vehicle. Kelly also remembered killing one of the aliens when her husband was led away by these dark, cloaked figures. The woman from the other car had started screaming, "Murderer!" Later on, Kelly was told by the aliens that this did not happen. Instead, it was an implanted memory used by the aliens to control the extreme state of anger that she was in.

As for the other car that Kelly had seen, she could now remember it in great detail. Investigator John Auchettl noted Kelly's description of it and started searching. He soon found this crucial link. There were three occupants in this vehicle that night, a married couple and a woman who was traveling with them. Each had a vague memory of the UFO encounter, but did not remember there was another car. Independent accounts were taken from the witnesses and they all matched with that of Kelly's. Even the description of the "alien" was identical. They were asked to draw the aliens and they all independently drew the same kind of beings. The husband, Andrew Cahill, had a vague memory of the incident, but it was the two women that the aliens seemed to be interested in. They remembered being taken into the craft where tests were performed on them. The encounter had left the two women with vaginal swelling and ring marks on their thighs.

Under hypnosis, the two women recalled a third car with a single male occupant. He had also been stopped on the same road by these aliens. Three years after the abduction, this lone driver was also traced. While he was reluctant to talk, he did give details of the UFO.

Now, there were three sets of unrelated witnesses giving the same story. Furthermore, the women had visible symptoms like vaginal swellings and physical marks on their bodies. Still not satisfied with this, skeptical UFO investigators studied the alleged landing sight of the UFO for radiation. Unexpected magnetic deviations were recorded at the sight.[39]

Close Encounters and Their Psychic Aftermath

In many cases, it has been found that after undergoing abduction the individual develops psychic abilities. This "gift" from the aliens enables people to know events in the future. It would give them an intuition that some experience was about to happen. In many people, it would come in the form of internal voices. In others, it would come as "visions" of the future. One such abduction occurred in Cheltenham, England, in 1942.

Cheltenham, England, February 1942

Tensions were high in England as Europe was in the middle of the Second World War. In Cheltenham, England, it was a bright, sunny afternoon and the streets were full of traffic and people. Eileen Arnold, seven months pregnant at the time, was returning home from a routine medical examination. She was in an unusually sensitive state of mind, an "emotional high," because she felt she was radiating out thoughts that others passing by seemed to pick up. Suddenly, something happened. The streets and the traffic began

---

[39] Randles, p. 52

to disappear and all sounds gradually faded as she lost her sense of time and space and her mind got tuned in to another reality. What became visible to her the next minute was a huge, flying object hovering right above the rooftops. It was large and oval with lights radiating from its holes. It moved slowly and smoothly, but, since both time and space seemed distorted, its speed was hard to judge. The spectacle seemed to have taken ages, but in real time and space it was a brief second.

The encounter changed Eileen's life. After this sighting, she started getting "visions" of the future. These experiences were what she believed to be messages coming from another dimension. She became a teacher after this incident, and dedicated years to educational services. In the end, however, she abandoned her profession and became a psychic counselor.

When Eileen's children were born, they also had the same powers. Her daughter, in particular, reported seeing a similar UFO with her mother when the daughter was thirteen. This happened in August 1975, when they were living in Malvern Hills, and Eileen suddenly had the urge to go out. They went to the balcony and saw an arrowhead object pass by. Again, the encounter left them both with a distorted sense of time and space.[40]

Nimes, France, April 10, 1952

It was the night of April 10 and twenty-four-year-old Rose was fast asleep in an outbuilding of her grandparent's country house.

---

[40] Randles, p. 18

Suddenly, the barking of the dogs awakened her. There was no one to be seen, but the dogs kept growling at an unseen presence. She stood up from the bed and followed the beasts outside.

They lead her to a stone building where she encountered four beings. While one of them looked human, three of them were much taller than seven feet, and one of them had a box with small buttons strapped on his chest. The man explained that he was a teacher and had an encounter with these beings in 1932. He was urged by these beings to go with them and, because he didn't have a family, he had agreed. For the last twenty years, he had lived with them in a faraway place. The time on their planet passed slower than on Earth, and, although he was forty-five-years-old (in Earth years), physically the man was still in his 20s. They invited Rose to go with them, but she refused to leave her four-year-old child. Instead, she gave them some literature (fashion magazines and a copy of *The Count of Monte Cristo* by Dumas). As a thank you gesture, the beings showed her their craft, and demonstrated its ability to make objects, such as rocks, float, and then de-materialize (as if being teleported into their ship).

After the encounter, Rose began to have psychic experiences. She would see visions of the future and hear voices in her head. Rose remained convinced that these came from the alien visitors.[41]

Implants

In June of 1992, Massachusetts Institute of Technology (MIT), one of the most respected scientific institutions in the world, organ-

---

[41] Randles, p. 17

ized an Abduction Study Conference that invited researchers from all across the United States to present their research on Close Encounters of the Fourth Kind. The event was hosted by MIT physicist Professor David E. Pritchard, with Professor John E. Mack as the co-chairman. Out of fifty-four researchers who presented their papers, twenty-three had a PhD or M.D. after their name, and twenty-one were professional psychiatrists or psychologists.

The most mind-blowing presentation was that of Pat Marcattilio, who revealed the discovery of "implants" or brain scan anomalies in two of the abductees.

In two of the abduction cases Marcattilio investigated, the aliens (as recalled by the abductees during a hypnosis session) had placed implants into the heads of the subjects. These were placed through their nasal cavities during two separate abductions. In order to verify these claims, Marcattilio organized Magnetic Resonance Imaging (brain scan) of both the subjects' heads at a neurological center in New York, and made one of the most startling discoveries of abduction UFOology. The brain scan located a 3mm zone of high intensity within the posterior sella turcica in one case, and another 3mm module in the left lobe of the pituitary gland in the other. This was not just physical evidence for the abduction, but also of the insertion of implants.

This was the beginning of what many UFO researchers describe as "the hunt for the implants." After this presentation, a great number of abductees were tested for implants. The tests included CAT scans, MRI, and x-rays. In three of the cases, implants were retrieved. In one case, an implant was sneezed out through the nose, and in another it started to come out through a skin eruption. Later

in 1995, several implants located through x-rays were surgically removed under controlled conditions. On August 19, 1995, a Houston-
based pediatrician, Dr. Roger Leir, removed two implants from the toe
of a female subject, and another from between the thumb and the
index finger of a man. The unusual pain experienced by the patients
suggested that the implants had been connected to the nervous system of the patients in order to receive data. Dr. Leir later explained
that before the operating procedure, an electromagnetic energy detector was used to examine the effected area. The resultant field was
so strong that the patient had to be taken out of the hospital and into
the parking area to check again in the absence of electromagnetic
energy sources. The same type of energy strength was detected.
After the surgery, when the removed implant had been placed in a container, it mysteriously stopped transmitting the field emissions.

The first implant turned out to be a metallic triangle with each
side 5 mm long. The other two were smaller, 2 x 4 mm and resembled
cantaloupe seeds. All three were wrapped in a very tight membrane
and fluoresced to a bright green color under black ultraviolet light.
Interestingly, they were all magnetic. Pathological analysis of the soft
tissues surrounding the insertion area revealed no inflammatory
cells or infiltrates and no fibrosis. This was extremely unusual because inflammation is the usual response to the presence of any foreign body in human tissue.[42]

Whoever inserted the implants had wrapped them in the
abductees' skin tissue, which prevented inflammation when the

---

[42] Hesseman, pp. 443-444

implant was inserted. This also explained the scoop marks found on different areas of the abductees' bodies. Furthermore, the implants were connected to the nervous system, obviously to acquire data. This was a technology far beyond human capability. Whoever placed those implants was not human. It was indeed the work of a superior intelligence.

Concluding Thoughts

The term "flying saucer" originated in 1947, and the term UFO (Unidentified Flying Object) came in to use much later. How do we explain alien encounters that happened before this era like that of Eileen Arnold in 1932? No one had either heard of the term "flying saucer" or "UFO" or read about one. Even if they are lying or imagining, why are their reports remarkably similar? Furthermore, why is it that the people mentioned in these reports cleared lie detector tests? How do we explain scars or surgical marks? The greatest proof has been implants which have been recovered from the bodies of people. Most of the UFO skeptics who ask such questions have only surface knowledge of the subject and are not aware of the seriousness of the research that has gone into the subject.

In the year 1992, the Roper Organization, an American demographic institution, carried out a Gallup poll on abductions. A total of eleven questions were asked, five with the aim of identifying probable abductees. They were:

1. Have you ever awakened paralyzed, sensing a strange figure or presence in the room?
2. Have you ever experienced an hour or more of "missing time"?

3. Have you ever felt like you were actually flying through the air without knowing why or how?

4. Have you ever seen unusual lights or balls of lights in the room without understanding what caused them?

5. Have you ever discovered puzzling scars on your body without remembering how and why they got there?

There were grounds to believe that anyone answering four of these with a "yes" was abducted in the past.

The results were mind-blowing. One in every 50 people met the profile of an abductee! What was more surprising was the fact that these tended to be people with above average education and were more socially or politically active than an average citizen. This basically tended to imply that abductions were happening on a far greater scale than we were ready to accept.

CHAPTER 3

RAPED BY ALIENS

Mysterious Cases of Phantom Pregnancies

One of the greatest mysteries of medical science is the "phantom pregnancy." These are pregnancies that appear without intercourse and disappear without an abortion. A woman gets up one morning feeling "strange." She knows something is different about her body, but does not know exactly what. In the days to come, she will stop menstruating, her breasts will enlarge and start retaining water, and she will start feeling pregnant. She may have been extra cautious with her birth control or not had sexual intercourse for a long time; nevertheless, the pregnancy symptoms start to appear. Obviously puzzled, she runs for a blood test and the results turn out positive. She is pregnant! Six to twelve weeks later, the menstrual cycles start again and the pregnancy disappears as mysteriously as it had come. There has been no abortion, miscarriage, or removal of fetal material, and yet it is gone. What the woman has undergone is a phantom pregnancy—medical science's greatest mystery.

Dr. David M. Jacobs is a PhD and an associate professor of History at Temple University. He is a leading authority on UFOs and one of the most knowledgeable people on the subject of abductions. In his study on alien abductions, he compiled firsthand accounts taken while the sixty abductees were under hypnosis. It turned out that some of his research subjects were women who had undergone phantom pregnancies. While these subjects consciously did not recall intercourse or an impregnation procedure, under hypnosis they recalled being taken into spacecrafts where, after a series of medical tests, they were injected with a fertilized egg. After their impregnation procedure, the memory of the abduction and impregnation was deleted and they were put back to the same spot from where they were taken. In the next few days, these women experienced a pregnancy without any conscious memory of the impregnation. After six weeks, the abduction occurred once again and this time the partially formed fetus was extracted. The most chilling thing about Dr. Jacob's research was the idea that what these women had carried in their wombs was an alien child—a genetic hybrid that was half human, half alien!

Decades before Dr. Jacobs carried out his research, a phantom pregnancy occurred in Westmoreland, New York, that left doctors and gynecologists totally baffled. It was the night of May 2, 1968, and Shane Kurz, a nineteen-year-old nursing aide, had seen a cigar-shaped object in the sky. After the sighting, Shane went to bed and fell into a deep, trance-like sleep. At around four in the morning, her mother found the girl missing and thought that she was probably in the washroom. When she checked again a little later, Shane was lying on top of her bed and covered in mud. The front door was open and a trail of footprints had formed from the doorway to her bed indicating that the girl had walked outside in her sleep.

In the next few days, Shane became very sick. Two red rings formed over her abdomen and she started getting powerful headaches. Her menstrual cycles stopped and did not reoccur until the next year. When they returned, their timing remained irregular for another four years. Doctors and gynecologists who studied her were left totally confused, because they had never encountered anything like this. Finally, it was hypnotic regression that brought back the missing memory.

Under hypnosis, Shane explained how she had been awakened by a light in the room. She walked outside where she was blinded by a blue light. Then she remembered the creatures with "off-white skins" that performed medical tests on her, including one in which a tube-like gadget was used to take ova samples. She was then told that she had been chosen for an experiment. She would give them a baby! She was obviously terrified and when the girl reacted hysterically, she was told that she would not remember anything, because they would make her forget what was to happen next.[43]

Many years later, a similar incident occurred. Karen Morgan was a thirty-eight-year-old businesswoman and the owner of a public relations firm. She wrote to Dr. David M. Jacobs and stated that she had an experience that might be related to his research on alien abductions. Dr. Jacobs interviewed Karen and finally ended up having over twenty sessions of hypnotherapy with her.

Under these hypnosis sessions, it was discovered that Karen had a memory of being in an operating room with naked people strapped

---

[43] Randles, p. 33

on operating tables.[44] She also was made to take off her clothes and was then strapped on an operating table. As always, the aliens communicated in a nonverbal manner and Karen was able to understand them without any verbal messages.

As more memories were uncovered, she had a flashback of being the subject of an advanced medical procedure. The surgical instrument was a long, round, tube-like device with an apparatus attached to one end. It had a bullet inside it. The aliens inserted the instrument into her body and the next feeling she had was that of the small object being fired into her. She began to scream and yelled to the aliens that she will have an abortion. She was told that she would not have any memory of it.[45] The next morning she woke up with no memory of the incident. She was surprised to find a gelatin-like substance between her thighs, which she washed away under the shower.[46]

Lynn Miller, another abductee studied by Dr. Jacobs, was abducted along with her son. She remembered how the two were separated and she was made to lie down on a table. A sharp needle was inserted through her navel and she described the needle as leaving "something" inside her. After the procedure, she was told by the beings that she had been "implanted."[47]

Janet Demerest, another one of Dr. Jacob's subjects, described the same kind of impregnation, but, in her case, it was a long, metallic instrument and it had been inserted through the vaginal

---

[44] Jacobs, p. 83
[45] Jacobs, p. 110
[46] Jacobs, p. 111
[47] Jacobs, p. 108

cavity. She had the feeling that "something" was being placed inside her. She was able to remember the object and described it as "a little, round thing."[48]

Egg Harvesting

Another procedure described under hypnosis by Dr. Jacobs' subjects was what he recognized as egg harvesting. This usually occurred before the impregnation and involved removing ova samples. Women recalled lying on tables while an alien would come and place his hand over the woman's abdomen. He presses right in the region above the ovaries. He uses the other hand to insert a variety of instruments into the vagina. The first instrument is a speculum-like device that opens up inside the vagina creating an opening large enough for the beings to work. Then the second instrument, described as a long and thin tube similar to a "daffodil stem," is then inserted. The abductees report that it goes very deep inside them. As the procedure goes on, women often report cramping or a twinge of pain and many know that something is being removed from inside them. They feel nauseated, dizzy, and weak. On some occasions, a liquid is injected (probably the same fluid that women later discover in the form of "gelatin-like" substance) which causes the women to "cramp." The procedures are painful, but in some cases the aliens use some kind of mind control to block the pain. This happened to Lynn Miller when the alien placed a hand on her head, and she could not feel the pain anymore.[49]

---

[48] Jacobs, p. 115
[49] Jacobs, p. 108

Fetal Extraction

Removing the partially formed fetus is the third procedure described by women who had undergone phantom pregnancies. Lynn Miller, who had been impregnated in an earlier abduction, was abducted once again. This time, the aliens used a long, black, speculum-like device with a "cup" or a container attached to the end. This instrument, as she described, was attached to another machine with buttons that lit up. The speculum-like device was inserted inside her, and she had the feeling that it was "tearing" something inside her. She kept yelling that it hurt, but the beings did not respond to her. They (aliens) pulled something right out of her and placed it in another container filled with water or some other fluid. Then she was made to look at the fetus. She did not want to see it, but they made her look at it and told her that it was her child and will be raised by them. When she complained that it was a part of her and they did not have the right to tear it out like that, she was told it was their right. The fetus was then placed inside the machine and Lynn Miller was told to get dressed.[50]

Anita Davis, another one of Dr. Jacobs' subjects, described a fetal extraction procedure that was performed while she was made to sit on a chair. It was described by the abductee to be an inclining chair that she would squat in. Her legs were bent like a frog with her feet planted firmly on a little foot platform underneath while her arms were placed on arm rests at the sides. When the fetus came out it fell into a glass-like thing. Anita Davis described its looks as what an

---

[50] Jacobs, p. 117

"early miscarriage" would look like. Throughout this procedure, Davis felt no pain nor was she afraid. She did feel a sense of relief after the removal.

Twenty-year-old Tracy Knapp wasn't that fortunate. A very long, needle-like instrument that she described as tiny "scissors" was inserted into her, and she felt them snipping. It felt like they were cutting away threads inside her body. During the procedure, a fluid was also placed inside her, which produced a "burning" sensation. During a hypnosis session, the subject broke down and started crying. "Yeah, they removed something out of me," she stated under hypnosis. "They removed like a, like a little baby or something. And they removed a sac or something. They removed the . . . but it's tiny, it's real tiny. It's not a baby."

At this point during the hypnosis, Dr. Jacobs asked her if it was an embryo.

"Yeah! It's like . . ." [51]

Before she could complete her reply, she remembered the "drawers." There were drawers nearby and the cylinder was being placed in one of these drawers. It was full of similar containers with other partially formed fetuses. She suddenly remembered seeing many such fetuses in there.[52]

Sperm Sampling, Envisioning, and Mind Control

Male abductees have also remembered procedures that are "reproductive" in nature. Sperm sampling is the most commonly

---

[51] Jacobs, p. 121

[52] Jacobs, p. 122

reported procedure in adult males. The aliens place a tube-like apparatus to take sperm samples. One end of this has a funnel-like device, and the other goes into a machine. Sometimes they place a metallic, cup-like instrument over the penis to extract sperm. Barney Hill[53] described a similar procedure. In order to facilitate the procedure, aliens often employ some kind of a mind control mechanism that makes the abductee think he is having sex with a human woman. The resulting visualization process is so realistic that in most cases the abductee cannot tell the difference between a real memory and that of envisioning.

Brazilian farmer Antonio Villas Boas underwent an experience that likely involved envisioning or mind control. It was mid-October 1957, and twenty-three-year-old Villas Boas was night plowing the fields near Sao Francisco de Sales. At around 1:00 a.m., a strange egg-shaped craft landed. The engine of Villas Boas' tractor went dead and his lights went out. He then describes being physically attacked by four masked beings that he described to be five feet tall. He was then taken into the landed craft where a blood sample was taken. Some kind of mysterious gas seeped in and filled the dimly lit room. The next thing he recalled was a beautiful, human female with white hair who communicated verbally. Intercourse followed at the end of which a sperm sample was taken. Villas was then brought back into the village. Later, Dr. Olavo Fontes examined Boas and was stunned to see that his patient was suffering from mild radiation sickness![54]

---

[53] See Chapter 4

[54] Randles, p. 26

Such cases are not rare, as both male and female abductees report having sex with a human-like creature. It is always difficult for UFO investigators to tell whether these are real experiences or "mind control" techniques meant to facilitate the sperm extraction or other sexual procedures. One theory is that they are "false memories" inserted later to block the abductee from remembering the actual event, which may be too frightening or unpleasant.

In 1957, Cynthia Appleton, a twenty-seven-year-old mother of two, remembers that she met with a "Greek athlete." He had blonde hair, blue eyes, and fair skin. His appearance was like a TV image but he would block out light. He would produce three dimensional television images in the air (a hologram—which was not invented in 1957!), and would give her information about the future that would always come true. He told her that his species were in touch with human scientists and together they were developing a "ray weapon." This turned out to be true; within a year, the government announced the invention of the laser beam.[55]

In the summer of 1958, the alien told Cynthia that she was pregnant. That also turned out to be true, as a doctor's appointment in the next few days confirmed. The visitor also reported the birth date, physical characteristics, and the weight of the baby. This information had been preserved on written record months before the birth. In the summer of 1959, Cynthia gave birth to a child of unusually close approximations.

---

[55] Readers should make a note of this as a detailed discussion on aliens exchanging technology to humans will follow in the latter part of the book

The interesting thing is that during his earlier visits, Cynthia had washed the visitors hand in water. Later, she found a piece of his skin in there. This was given to a Dr. Dale who immediately had a Manchester University biologist examine it under an electron microscope. The analysis revealed that the skin was not human. It resembled that of a pig![56] This suggested that whatever it was that was visiting Cynthia was not human, and that he was there in flesh and blood. But was he actually like a "Greek athlete"? Or was Cynthia made to see him that way? This question remains unanswered.

Hybrid Babies

Fourteen-year-old James Austino had undergone an abduction earlier for the purpose of sperm collection. In another abduction later on, Austino remembered standing in a large room that had glass tubes running straight up to the ceiling. These tubes contained a liquid, which appeared to be illuminated in a crystal-blue color with lights shining from below. With the whole room full of these tubes, the place had the feel of a giant fish tank. In these "fish tanks," Austino saw small hamster-like creatures with wires attached to them. Curled up in a fetal position, they floated in their liquid environment. Austino moved in to get a closer look. The creatures were very similar to human fetuses with the exception of their eyes which were bluish-black. Austino said he had seen around seventy such things just floating in there. All of the tubes went into a giant monitoring unit—a life support system that produced gurgling and bubbling sounds.

---

[56] Randles, pp. 28-29

Anita Davis described rectangular fish tanks. It was a large room that was brightly lit with a glass wall. She stood in the middle of the room looking into these tanks at what appeared to be hybrid babies in different phases of their development. Kept on life support, they continued growing in a semi-liquid kind of environment. She described over a hundred such babies, some larger and more developed than the others. The alien pointed at one and told her "this one is yours."[57]

Karen Morgan was not sure whether the babies were in liquid or not. She saw them from behind a glass panel lying in boxes. "They are breeding us," she had said to Dr. Jacobs.[58] They were stored in there in different phases of development. There was no movement and no sound, but she knew they were alive. It was not something she wanted to remember.

Barbara Archer, who was abducted from Ireland in 1988, was taken into a room with rows of babies. There were about twenty placed in two rows of ten. Their grayish skin looked very different from human skin and their arms seemed longer. Their overall texture struck Barbara as very fragile. They had an unhealthy look to them.[59]

Jill Pinzarro felt a sudden affection toward the baby. She was handed the baby and she held it close to her. Unlike Barbara Archer's, who had described the baby to be a grayish color, Pinzarro found it white. She felt that the baby needed rhythm, so she walked him around. Soon, the baby was taken away from her.

---

[57] Jacobs, p. 189
[58] Jacob, p. 158
[59] Jacobs, p. 16

Generally, seeing the baby was not a pleasant experience. The women found it frightening. It did not look like an alien baby, nor did it look like a human one. Its head was unusually large and its body was described as thin. It did not have baby fat like a human child. Its gray or white skin was described as almost translucent. When women held it, it did not have the moving reflex of a human baby. It was passive and looked lifeless, but women knew it was alive. Abductees initially described it as unhealthy, but after holding it for a while it became slightly more energetic.

Conclusion

The word "flying saucer" was first used in 1947. The term UFO came about even later. If stories of alien contact are myths inspired by modern science fiction, how should we explain cases of alien contact that happened before 1947? Furthermore, we have to acknowledge that the human mind's ability to "imagine" things is very limited. If we look at science fiction films of the 1970s or even old episodes of Star Trek, we see the interiors of spacecrafts littered with bizarre-looking mechanical junk. We have superior technology in our houses today. If abductees were imagining all this, their fantasies would also be full of out-dated mechanical junk. Instead, when we analyze cases of abduction, people under hypnosis talk about laser surgeries, reverse magnetism, genetic cross breeding, and things that have only started to make sense recently. How could people all of a sudden just "imagine" things that even science fiction writers of the early 1970s could not come up with? And how should we explain to ourselves the medical evidence, the implants, and surgical marks? When all factors are taken into consideration, no matter how believable it may sound, the most probable conclusion is that we are being experimented upon by a superior intelligence.

CHAPTER 4

LAND OF THE ASTRONAUT GODS

Has the Earth Been Visited?

Between southern France and northern Spain lie the pre-historic caves of the Pyrenees. In the Stone Age, between 30,000 and 10,000 B.C., small colonies of cave dwellers inhabited the place. These settlers spent a great deal of time creating rock paintings and carvings that can still be found inside these cave complexes.

The late Professor Leroi-Gourhan, an academic in the field of pre-historic art, had earned the title of the "Cave Man" for the countless hours he had spent in these caves studying the ancient artwork. With a pencil and paper, he would spend long hours in these moist and chilly caves, reproducing with his hands, sketches of what ancient cave dwellers painted. Today, even after his death, his reproductions of prehistoric art are studied at all major universities across the world.

This priceless prehistoric art is of great academic value as it depicts people engaged in the every day activities of their lives thousands of years ago. Browsing through these cave paintings, one can easily make out hunters with spears, animals of different kinds, bison, horses, deer, goats, and flying saucers! That's right, flying saucers. When the French ethnologist, Aime Michel, saw Professor Leroy-Gourhan's reproductions of prehistoric cave art, he could not believe his eyes. Among all the things depicted, the most striking were floating disc-shaped objects painted in the sky. "In the caves there are up to forty different types of strange objects resembling in an astounding manner the manifestations in our skies which, during the last twenty years, have been called UFOs, and which according to Condon report do not exist," stated Michel in 1969.[60]

Rock paintings of these disc-shaped objects were found in seventeen prehistoric caves, including Altamira, Lascaux, Pech Merle, and Les Trois Freres. The question that this prehistoric art raises is whether these disc-shaped objects represent the same phenomenon we see in our skies today as UFOs? When everything else in these paintings is real (bison, goats, horses, etc) is there also a reality behind these disc-shaped objects floating in air? If not, then why would prehistoric cavemen, who have painted everything else from real life, all of a sudden have the urge to paint saucers in the air with long trails behind them? If UFOs are nothing more than a modern myth, how could people living thousands of years before the space age just "visualize" it? And not just visualize the phenomenon, but also visualize it with such accuracy that we can make out the aerodynamic shape and the exhausts from the engines?

[60] Hesseman, p. 226

Annunaki: The Gods of Sumeria

Between 3800 B.C. and 2000 B.C., in the southern region of what is now the present day Iraq, existed the city-states of Sumer (pronounced "shoomer"). With their temples, palaces, hospitals, and parliaments, the Sumerians were the earliest examples of an urban culture. What was amazing about these people was the fact that this magnificent urbanization sprang up from nothing. There were no early stages in their development.

Modern archeology still cannot answer the question of "Where did Sumerians get this advanced knowledge?" If Sumerians themselves were asked, their ancient texts state that they acquired their knowledge from their gods, the "Annunaki." The literal meaning of the word Annunaki is "those who descended on the earth from the skies." A very fitting name for extraterrestrial visitors, isn't it?

Further study of ancient Sumerian texts reveals that the gods that Sumerians worshipped traveled through the skies in heavenly vehicles called "Mu" or "Din-Gin." They would come down upon every town in which there was a temple dedicated to their worship and perform miracles for their worshippers. Their temple, a pyramid-shaped building, was an abode where priests regularly provided these "gods" with young girls or young men (in the case of Goddess Ishtar or Innana).[61] The question that comes to mind is that if the gods were aliens from outer space, what would they do with the human males or females? Were the gods from heavens using these subjects to perform genetic experiments?

---

[61] Hesseman, p. 237

Further analysis of the same Sumerian texts reveals that the gods would mate with men and produce creatures that were half-men, half-gods. The mention of such "hybrid" people is found in the great historical find, *The Epic of Gilgamesh*. The epic was a sensational discovery made in the hills of Kuyundjik in the beginning of the 19th century. What archeologists had discovered were twelve clay tablets that belonged to the library of Assyrian king, Assurbanipal. Written in Akkadian, the clay tablets documented the heroic tale of the victorious hero "Gilgamesh."

It is an established fact today that the original version of the epic comes from the Sumerians. According to the tablets, the hero of the story was Gilgamesh; he was a ruler of the town of Uruk and a man unmatched in strength and beauty. Pilgrims who came to his city trembled at his sight for they had never seen his type. What was different about Gilgamesh was that he was a hybrid species of half-man and half-god. The tablets described him as two-thirds man and one-third god.

According to the same tablets, another such figure created by the gods was Enkidu. The tablets describe him as a total opposite of Gilgamesh. Unlike Gilgamesh, Enkidu was ugly and hideous looking with the whole of his body covered with hair. He would wear animal skin instead of clothes, eat grass, and drink water with the cattle. When Gilgamesh found out about this creature, he ordered that Enkidu be given a beautiful woman to mate with. Thus, Enkidu spent six days and six nights with a beautiful woman. After this cross breeding, we read that the gods descended and seized Enkidu![62]

---

[62] Von Daniken, pp. 62-64

Later on in the story we read about how Enkidu was taken into the skies by the gods. He flew with the gods for hours, and this is how he has described the earth as seen from above. Notice the details of the aerial view of the earth.

> "He said to me, 'Look down at the land. What does it look like? Look at the sea. How does it seem to you?' And the land was like a mountain and the sea was like a lake. And again he flew for four hours and said to me, 'Look down at the land. What does it look like? Look at the sea. How does it seem to you?' And the earth was like a garden and the sea was like the water channel of the gardener. And he flew higher for another four hours and then spoke, 'Look down at the land. What does it look like? Look at the sea. How does it seem to you?' And the land looked like porridge and the sea was like a water trough."[63]

Could this account solely be the product of pure imagination or had someone actually seen the earth from a higher altitude? Today, we live in the age of air travel. Most of us have seen the ground from a higher altitude, either from a plane or through photographs, television, etc. How difficult would it be for us to come up with this description if these recent electronic mediums did not exist?

The other thing worth considering is that writing did not exist at the time the Epic was documented. Writing as we know today was not technically possible since paper had not been invented. Information had to be carved on clay tablets, which as one can imagine, must have been a laborious task. Due to the huge effort involved, only very important pieces of information would be noted. Why would ancient

---

[63] Epic of Gilgamesh as quoted in Chariots of Gods, p. 64

Sumerians preserve a nonsensical fairy tale unless it had some real-world significance?

Gods of Egypt

Not far from southern Iraq laid the remains of another civilization. In the middle of the desert with its elaborate architecture, expressive statues, and a skyline dominated by towering pyramids, we find another advanced urban culture—ancient Egypt. The ancient Egyptians left behind an advanced calendar, complicated sewage system, enormous temples, perfectly carved stone statues, mummified pharaohs, and, above all, colossal pyramids built to an impossible mathematical precision. Just like the Sumerians, this rather mystical culture had no early stages or prerequisites. It had no recognizable prehistory. It arose from nothing!

The interesting thing to note in this region, as Erich Von Daniken points out in his book *Chariots of the Gods?* is the scarcity of agriculture. Since small strips of agricultural land existed along the Nile, how is it possible that this glorious civilization, with an estimated 50 million people,[64] existed in the middle of the desert with no visible food sources? We cannot imagine Canada, a country with a population of 30 million, surviving solely on the produce growing along the river Nile, so how can we accept the explanation that a thriving civilization of 50 million survived on it?

Furthermore, in recent movies and paintings we see slaves dragging stone blocks on wooden rollers to construct the pyramids.

---

[64] Von Daniken, p. 94

Yet, it seems very unlikely that the ancient Egyptians would cut down the few trees that grew along the Nile and use them as rollers, for those were desperately needed food sources. Even if we accept the explanation that wooden rollers were used to transport huge blocks of concrete, the pace of work would have been extremely slow. At the amazing rate of ten stone blocks piled on each other a day (which, even for a modern construction contractor seems to be an extraordinary daily piece rate), the two-and-a-half-million stone pyramid would have taken 664 years![65]

More mysterious is the fact that around 2,500,000 blocks of stone were cut, dressed, and fitted together to the nearest thousandth of an inch. Even if the stonemasons, while cutting the stone, made an error of no greater than 1mm in each block, with 2,500,000 blocks, the alignment of the whole pyramid would have been out by over 8000 feet! What we have are perfect pyramids thousands of years old, looking at us and asking, "Do you really think we were made by humans?"

The question becomes more important if we consider the fact that the height of the pyramid multiplied by a thousand million equals the distance from the earth to the sun. A coincidence? How about the fact that a meridian running through the pyramids divides the continents and the oceans into two exactly equal halves?[66] How could the ancient place the structures on the world map in this manner unless some aerial view of the earth existed? Readers should remember the aerial account of Enkidu in the "Epic of Gilgamesh."

---

[65] Von Daniken raised this question in "Chariots of the Gods," pp. 98-99

Archeology again has no conclusive answer as to where the Egyptians got their advanced knowledge. If Egyptians themselves are asked, their texts mention cosmic gods that sailed the skies in heavenly barques and came down to perform miracles for the devotees. In their religious rituals, the Egyptians would take statues of these gods down the Nile in boats. The interesting thing is that Sumerians were not the only people who believed that gods mated with men, as ancient Egyptians believed their pharaohs to be the descendents of the gods as well![67]

An interesting discovery was made during the 19th century excavations at Thebes. What appeared to be a report written on a papyrus fragment turned out to be the oldest UFO-related government document in recorded history! For years, it remained in the private collection of Professor Albert Tulli of the Vatican Museum. It was only after his death that his brother Monsignore Gustavo permitted researcher Boris, Prince of Rachewiltz, to translate the text. The partially destroyed document from the court scribe of Pharaoh Thutmosis III (1483–1450 B.C.), reads as follows:

"In the third winter month of the year 22 (1462 B.C. according to modern researchers), and at the sixth hour of the day, the scribes in the House of Life noticed that a ball of fire came out of the sky. It had no head but the breath from its mouth had an obnoxious smell. Its body was one rood long (approximately 135 feet), one rood broad, and it had no voice. The hearts of the scribes were filled with fear and they fell down on the floor . . . (fragment destroyed) . . . they informed the pharaoh. His

---

[67] Hesseman, p. 239

Majesty ordered . . . was investigated . . . and he meditated over what had happened and what had been written down on papyri in the House of Life. Now, after a few days had passed, behold! There were these things that became more numerous in the sky than ever before. They appeared with more brightness than the sun, and stretched out till the borders of the four corners of the world . . . Powerfully they stood these balls of fire in the sky. The army of the pharaoh watched them with the pharaoh himself in their midst. It was after the evening meal. Then, the balls of fire rose higher up in the sky toward the south. A wonder that was unknown since the establishment of this nation and the pharaoh ordered the incense should be offered so that peace could reign on the earth . . . and whatever had happened was to be written according to the order of the pharaoh, in the annals of the House of Life . . . so that it would remain in memory forever."[68]

Hinduism: The UFO Connection

At around 3000 years B.C., another civilization had sprung up in what is now India (and areas of Pakistan). The inhabitants of the region, Hindus (people of Indus), had access to certain knowledge that we have discovered only recently. In ancient Sanskrit, astronomical text Surya-siddhanta, the diameter of the earth is described to be 1600 yojanas and the diameter of the moon as 480 yojanas. The value of a yojana is argued to be five miles. Given this value per yojana, these ancient people calculated the diameter of the earth to be 800 miles and the moon to be 2400 miles.[69] It's not a pin-point

---

[68] Hesseman, pp. 239-241
[69] Thompson, p. 215

figure, but it's miraculous bearing in mind that the ancient people had no access to the modern scientific instruments that we have used in recent years to come up to more or less the same figures.

Modern archeology again fails to answer how these people (living thousands of years ago) could acquire such advanced knowledge. The remarkable thing is that just like Sumerians and Egyptians, the Hindus also believed in gods that came from the skies and brought with them advanced knowledge and technology. These gods are mentioned repeatedly in *Bhagavata Purana*, *Mahabharta*, and *Ramayana*—the three most important works in Hindu tradition. *Bhagavata Purana*, according to modern researchers, dates back to the ninth century A.D. and *Mahabharta* and *Ramayana* go as far back as the fifth to sixth century A.D. Hindu tradition, however, dates all three texts back to at least 3000 years B.C. (around the same time period of Sumerians). Modern researchers agree that these texts incorporate material much older than the time period in which they were compiled.

While going through these ancient writings, we find mention of vehicles called "Vimanas" in which gods visited the land. The Vimanas were heavenly vehicles (dome-shaped in most cases) that would fly individually or in formation, hover over hills and water, and become invisible. The flight characteristics and visual description of Vimanas seem remarkably similar to modern UFOs.

In *Bhagvata Purana*, we read about a flying machine built for King Salva by a person known as Maya Dhanava.

"This airplane (Vimana) occupied by Salva was very mysterious. It was so extraordinary that sometimes many airplanes would appear to be in the sky and sometimes there were apparently none. Sometimes the plane was visible and sometimes not visible, and the warriors of the Yadu dynasty were puzzled about the whereabouts of the peculiar airplane. Sometimes they would see the airplane (Vimana) on the ground, sometimes flying in the sky, sometimes resting on the peak of a hill, and sometimes floating on the water. The wonderful airplane flew in the sky like a whirlwind firebrand; it was not steady even for a moment."[70]

Whirlwind firebrand? Does it not sound like the recent description of UFOs? The most interesting thing about this account is that in Hindu mythology, Maya Dhanava, the builder of this magnificent heavenly vehicle, is believed to be a native of the lower planetary system![71] He had come from a planet known as Talatala.[72]

In the tenth canto of *Bhagavata Purana*, we are left astonished as we read how King Salva destroyed the Lord Krsna's grand city of Dvaraka by aerial bombardment from this magnificent Vimana.

"Salva besieged the city with a large army, O, best of Bharatas decimating the outlying parks and gardens, the mansions along with the observatories, towering gateways and surrounding walls, and also the public recreational areas. From his excellent airship, he threw down a torrent of weapons, including stones, tree trunks, thunderbolts, snakes, and hailstones. A fierce whirlwind arose and blanketed all directions with dust."[73]

---

[70] Thompson, pp. 224-225
[71] Hesseman, p. 235.b
[72] Thompson, p. 227
[73] Thompson, p. 226

The story goes on to tell us how this invisible Vimana was destroyed by Lord Krsna, who used a "sound-seeking arrow."

"I took my glittering bow, best of the Bharatas, and cut with my arrows the heads of the gods' enemies on the Saubha. I shot well-robed arrows, which looked like poisonous snakes, high flying and burning arrows from my Sarnga at King Salva. Then the Saubha became invisible, O prosperer of Kuru's language concealed by wizardry and I was astounded. The bands of the Danavas, with grimacing faces and disheveled heads, screeched out loud as I held my ground, great king. I quickly lay on an arrow which killed by seeking out sound to kill them, and the screeching subsided. All the Danavas who had been screeching lay dead, killed by the blazing sun-like arrows that were triggered by sound."[74]

Blazing sun-like arrows that are triggered by sound? In the modern age, we are all familiar with sonar-guided missiles that can be aimed at a sound source miles away, beyond visual range. How could people living thousands of years ago perceive such technology? The text also goes on to say that this magnificent arrow killed all the Danavas, a race of intelligent beings in Hindu mythology who were on board the Vimana. This tends to suggest that the craft was piloted by nonhuman beings.

Another ancient work of Hindu literature is the historical epic *Ramayana*. In this story, we read that long ago a country by the name Lanka (present day Sri Lanka according to most experts) was occupied by beings called "Raksasas" who had certain mystical

------
[74] Thompson, p. 228

powers. They could change their physical appearances, fly through the air, and snatch people away. Ravana, the king of these beings, snatched Sita, the wife of Lord Rama and imprisoned her in Lanka.[75]

As we go through the story, we read about the frequent chases that were carried out in Vimanas. We read that Rama, in order to save his wife, acquired a Vimana that was big, with a split deck and many chambers with windows. It had its own driving power, and at Rama's command would ascend into the clouds making tremendous noise. In fact, it was this very apparatus in which Rama crossed the ocean and reached the island of Lanka from India. There, his enemy Ravana, who waited for him in another Vimana, confronted him. It was "glowing bright and frightening, throwing a jet of flame in the summer night, like a comet in the sky surrounded by huge clouds."[76]

Read the description once again. It was a brightly glowing flying object that would release a jet of flame at night?

Mahabharta also documents an encounter between the Pandava hero Arjun and a goddess by the name "Ulupi." The story begins when Arjuna is exiled for accidentally intruding on his brother, Yudhistira, and their common wife, Draupadi. He goes to the river Ganges and participates in a sacrificial ritual being carried out by the sages.

"When his residence was thus crowded with divinity, the darling son of Pandu (Arjuna) and Kunti then went down into the Ganges water to be consecrated for holy rite. Taking his ritual bath and worshipping his

[75] Thompson, pp. 218 and 251
[76] Ramayana as quoted by Hesseman, p. 235

forefathers, Arjuna, happy to take his part in the rite of fire, was rising out of the water, O King when he was pulled back by Ulupi, the virgin daughter of the serpent king, who could travel about at her will and was now within those waters. Holding unto him she pulled him into the land of the Nagas, into her father's house."[77]

After his abduction by Ulupi, Arjun had a sexual encounter with the Naga woman and was then returned. An interesting fact we should be aware of is that in Hindu mythology, Nagas are a race of intelligent beings that come from the planetary system Bila-svarga, and also occupy parallel realities in our world![78]

In the same book, another encounter with a demonic female being is described, and this time the contactee is King Doryodhana. The story tells us that the king was captured by a group of Ghandarvas (who, like Nagas and Danavas are another race of intelligent beings). When Arjuna finds out about his disappearance, he uses his connection with the gods to free Doryodhana, on the grounds that he was his relative and a fellow human being. After his release, the proud ruler felt humiliated at being rescued by a person he had considered unequal and scorned as his enemy. Thus, he decides to commit suicide by starving himself to death. Upon hearing this, the "Danavas" (another intelligent life form) summon a beautiful woman to fetch Doryodhana. This woman, a type of demonic being known as krtya, comes to Doryodhana and transports the king to the world of Danavas. Danavas then convinced the king to spare himself and promise him aid against

[7] Thompson, p. 240
[78] Thompson, p. 241

Pandavas in battle. They also promise him the blood of Arjuna, the very man who had saved him. After agreeing to their terms, the king is then returned to the same spot where he was fasting to death. The same krtya woman brought him down, and then disappeared. Doryodhana returns to his senses and thinks that it had all been a dream. He is left with only one thought, and that is that he will destroy the Pandus in battle.[79]

Reading the Hindu texts we also realize that the devotees made sacrifices to these "gods." *Bhagavata Purana* describes how another ruler, King Yudishtira, organized a sacrificing ritual in which "demigods," described as "rulers of various planets"[80] came down and participated. It goes on to say that "the domes of the city's palaces shone even as the domes of the beautiful aircraft which hover above the city."[81]

Vimana's, the mystical vehicles of the gods, have occupied a central part in Hindu mythology. Yet, the most detailed description of these vehicles is found in a text known as *Vimanic Shastra*. Interestingly, the name "Vimanika Shastra" literally means "The Book of Space Travel." Maharishi Baradhvaja, the writer of this ancient text, according to modern researchers, lived at around 700 B.C. Indian tradition dates him as far back as 3000 years B.C. In his manuscript, Vimana, the vehicle of the gods is described in the following words:

---

[79] Thompson, p. 243
[80] Bhagavata Purana as quoted by Hesseman, p. 236

- "An apparatus having the mechanism to generate its own power. It moves equally well on the ground, in water, and in the air. It can fly through the air from place to place, country to country, and planet to planet."

- It has the secret means of making itself motionless or invisible. It can over hear distant conversations and other noises in enemy-flying craft, obtain pictures of the insides of inimical aircraft, determine their course, and make persons in the inimical craft unconscious."

- "It can make itself 'glow' in the air because the electric energy collides with the outside wind." (A phenomenon we recognize today as ionization).[82]

The Puranas also claim that at the time there were 400,000 people in the universe and that every planet was inhabited either materially or on an ethereal plane. In fact, the text also goes on to say that it was these "visitors" from other planets that brought down the spiritual knowledge of Hinduism.[83] Readers should make a note of this, as a detailed discussion on the topic will follow in chapter 8.

Other Accounts

About thirty miles from Mexico City in South America lay the pyramid fields of Teotihuacan. Thousands of years ago, the Mayan civilization that inhabited this region began constructing their pyramid-shaped temples. Today, it is obvious that all their buildings

---

[81] Bhagvata Purana as quoted by Hesseman, p. 236
[82] Hesseman, p. 234

were laid out according to advanced astronomical plans. They knew about Uranus and Neptune and calculated the solar and Venusian years to four decimal places.

Their knowledge, according to the Mayan legends, came from gods that came from the skies. One particular god named "Quetzelcoatl" had come from an unknown land and brought with him very wise laws. He taught people science, arts, tradition, and, under his guidance, corn crops grew as high as a man's height and cotton grew already colored.

Was Quetzelcoatl, the Mayan god, an alien visitor? The thing to note here is that Mayan priests, just like their Egyptian and Sumerian counterparts, guarded their knowledge with an uncompromising secrecy. Regarding the pyramid field, the oldest Teotihaucan text tells us that the gods assembled in the area and took council about man even before *Homo sapiens* existed![84]

Concluding Thoughts

We live in a land of the astronaut gods. Throughout this planet, we find remains of cultures (some still existing today) that worshipped cosmic gods that descended from the heavens. We find stories of gods that mated with humans and left behind "demigods" that ruled the earth. If these were just written accounts, we could have explained them as nonsensical folklore of the ancient. But throughout the earth, we find architectural wonders that are

---

[83] Bhagavata Purana as quoted by Hesseman, p. 236
[84] Von Daniken Chariots of the Gods, p. 118

impossible to build even with the most sophisticated technology.

There are certain things strikingly common in the Sumerians, the Egyptians, and the Hindus:

- Their interest in outer space! All three of these civilizations had well-developed calendars and advanced astronomy.
- They left behind mind-blowing mathematical calculations and architectural achievements.
- They all sought their gods in the skies!
- Their gods mated with humans to produce a race that ruled these cultures.

Even if we bless the ancient with a wild imagination, how can we explain the striking similarity of their beliefs?

We can't help but be amazed when we look at ancient Egyptians. It seemed as if the whole civilization generation after generation spent their entire time and resources erecting pyramids. What madness drove these people to spend their lives building these colossal structures whose only purpose is to preserve the dead? How did they achieve the magnificent architectural masterpiece that seems almost impossible even to modern builders?

French novelist Jules Verne is accepted today as the father of modern science fiction. In his book *Twenty Thousand Leagues Under the Sea* (1870), this eighteenth-century writer perceived submarines before they were technologically possible. In *Around the World in Eighty Days*, he perceived flight before it was technologically possible. In *From the Earth to the Moon*, he perceived space travel. In none of his works was he able to imagine a sonar-guided missile! Today's submarines are equipped with sound-seeking torpedoes that pick a distant sound in the ocean and follow it for miles, but the concept was far too advanced for the eighteenth-century novelist. "Nautilus," his imaginary submarine in *Twenty Thousand Leagues Under the Sea*, was equipped with a giant razor blade! How could the writers of Mahabharta in 3000 B.C. visualize a blazing sound-seeking arrow, which is something that the father of modern science fiction, Jules Verne, could not imagine two centuries ago?

All of these questions are answered if we open our minds to the possibility that we have had visitors. For thousands of years, the human race has been a subject of medical experimentation by an extraterrestrial species—an intelligent alien life form that has been visiting the earth since its very beginnings. Ancient civilizations worshipped the visitors as "gods" and offered sacrifices to them. They presented the gods with human subjects that were used in cross-breeding experiments. In return, the gods rewarded them with advanced knowledge and technology, whose evidence we see today in the form of pyramids, architectural remains, and mind-blowing, mathematical calculations.

PART II

Islam and UFOs!

Religion (which in this context is Islam) and the UFO phenomenon are like two pieces of a giant jigsaw puzzle. If separated, they both fall outside the realms of conventional logic, but when put side by side they complete the whole picture. For more than half a century, Western UFO researchers have wrestled with questions like exactly what are UFOs? Where do they come from? What interest do they have in us and why are governments concealing information regarding them?

The answers to these questions lies in the second piece of the puzzle—the piece we will examine now. This portion of our book begins in another time, in another place, and in a land presently known as the Kingdom of Saudi Arabia. What you are about to read here will blow your mind.

CHAPTER 5

"IQRA"

Mystery of the Islamic Scriptures

In the mid-fifth century, pre-Islamic Arabia was nothing more than a nomadic land inhabited mostly by wandering tribes. Small cities had sprung up near water sources, but their purpose was only to serve as resting places for trade caravans. Since sustenance in the region was scarce both for men and beasts, tempers were always high. Theft and robbery was no crime in the eyes of these nomadic Arabs. Many of the passing caravans had to pay them "protection money" to let them go through the land. Theirs was a social structure based on tribal loyalties and revenge. If one person of a clan was killed, the whole clan sought revenge. Some of the tribal feuds went on for generations with many being killed on both sides.

Religiously speaking, these people were pagans who worshipped deities carved of wood and stone. Rituals of magic and sorcery were common, and blood sacrifices (of animals) were offered to the idols. A man's strength, influence, and earning potential was measured by the number of sons he had, for it was the male child that was seen as the potential contributor to the economy. Female infants were generally perceived as bad luck, because in the eyes of pre-Islamic Arabs, they were merely mouths to feed. Some clans had also adopted the custom of burying female infants alive. This horrible ritual has been described very clearly by Gen. A. I. Akram in his book, *The Sword of Allah*:

> "The father would let the child grow up normally until she was five to six years old. He would then tell her that he would take her for a walk, and then dress her up as if for a party. He would then take her out of the town or settlement to a sight that was already dug for her. He would make the child stand on the edge of the grave and the child, quite unaware of her fate and believing that her father had brought her out for a picnic, would look eagerly at him wondering when the fun would start. The father would then push her into the grave, and as the child cried to her father to help her out, he would hurl large stones at her crushing the life out of her tender body. When all movement had ceased in the bruised and broken body of the poor victim, he would fill the grave with earth and return home. Sometimes he would brag about what he had done."[85]

Beside women, the most oppressed segment of the society was the slaves that were brought from Africa. Owned by the ruling Arab elite, they were deprived of their fundamental human rights.

Reform

Original sources describe him as a handsome man with dark eyelashes, a hooked nose, and long hair that ended in curls just

---

[85] Akram, p. 10

below his ears. Though not exceptionally tall, he was strongly built with broad shoulders and very large, powerful hands. His name was Muhammad-ibn-Adullah. Today, we recognize him as "Prophet Muhammad".

His father had died before he was born. Since the tribal custom prevented a minor from inheriting his father's wealth, he had been deprived of his inheritance. It was not very long when his mother also died and with no one to look after him, he was adopted by his grandfather Abdul-Mutalib. After the death of his grandfather, his custody went to his uncle, Abu Talib. As a boy, he tended flock which was something most boys of his age did. Even in his early age he had a keen observation for things.

In the center of Mecca stood Ka'ba, a dark, stone structure originally built by Abraham for the purpose of monotheistic worship. Meccans had now placed wood and stone idols in it that not only attracted the locals, but pilgrims from other parts of the regions who brought trade and revenue into the city. Since Muhammad's grandfather was the guardian of Ka'ba, young Muhammad had been inside the place many times, often wondering why people bow down to wood and stone.

Since his early days, he had developed an honest reputation, and, thus, by the time he reached his youth, he had earned the trust and confidence of a great number of people. In the wide social circle of Mecca, he was known as Sadiq (the honest one) and Amin (one that can be trusted).

His reputation of fair dealing and honesty reached a business woman by the name of Khadija who hired him to take her trade caravans to neighboring lands and deal on her behalf. Soon his sincerity, mannerisms, and honesty not only won Khadija's confidence, but also her heart. She proposed to him and he accepted, though she was twenty years older than his twenty-five. In spite of the age gap between the two, their marriage was a perfect one.

In his early days, he had enjoyed wrestling, horse riding, and fencing, but now that he was growing older, his attention was drawn toward more sober issues in the Arab culture. He would often walk the deserted streets at night all alone pondering over tribal vendetta's, racial prejudices, treatment of women, and orphans. Finally, he began to withdraw to the Hira Mountains where he would sit in a cave all night in deep thought and meditation.

It was during one of these lonely nights that Muhammad had an experience. The details of this experience are complex, but traditions tell us that he was addressed by a presence that called itself Archangel Gabriel. The angel said to him:

"IQRA!"

Recite

IQRA . . . BISMI RABI KAL LAZZI KHALAQ

Recite . . . in the name of thy Lord who created

KHALAQ –AL –INSANA – MIN - ALAQ

Who created human from something that clings

IQRA! WA RABUKAL AKRAM

Recite! Your Lord is the most noble

ALLAZI ALAMA BIL QALAM

Who taught by the pen

ALLAMAL INSAANA MA'LAM YA'LAM

Who taught human what he did not know."

This was the beginning of Quranic revelation, which he continued to receive for the next twenty years. The messages had an authoritative tone as if the author of the book (God) was addressing Muhammad and the entire human kind in the first person. Linguistically, it was a masterpiece beyond anything ever produced in Arabic.

Initially, he preached the revelation only to a trusted few, but when he came out in public his message was met with fierce opposition. He was preaching the message of social change, which was something totally unacceptable to the tribal lords. In spite of the social and moral decay of their society, the Arabs took great pride in their traditions and had no tolerance for a reformer. Thus, during the initial stages, they persecuted his followers and harassed him; some even tried to bribe him but when nothing worked; they planned to kill him.

After surviving an assassination attempt, the prophet escaped to a town called Medina whose inhabitants had converted to Islam and were now welcoming him as their political leader. This was the politicizing of Islam because after his arrival in Medina, the revelations that he received began focusing more on political and social issues rather than an individual relationship with God. From this point onward, Islam was not just a religion but a political ideology that was promising to take over the whole of Arabia. As the revelations progressed, the prophet's companions memorized the text and recited them.

The wordings of the scriptures were also taken down by scribes in his guidance.

The evidence of this comes from the Quran itself:

"By no means! Indeed it is a message of instruction

Therefore whoever wills, should remember

On leaves held in held in honor

Exalted, purified in the hands of scribe Noble and Pious."

(Sura 18: Verses 11-16)

These series of revelations that the Prophet received for over twenty years were given the name Quran or Koran meaning "utterances" (Quran). In order to triple check on the content, the whole of the Quran was read during the month of Ramadhan in the presence of the Prophet's companion who knew the whole scripture by heart. The tradition has continued today.

Though the writing of the Quran had been going on even before the Prophet had migrated to Medina, it was not until the death of Prophet Muhammad that the first complete hardcopy was compiled. Abu Bakar, the first Caliph of Islam, asked Prophet Muhammad's head scribe, Zaid ibn Thabith, to make a complete hardcopy and this he did. It is also known that the second Caliph of Islam, Hazrat Umer, ordered a completed volume, which he presented to his daughter, the Prophet's widow, Hafsa. Finally, during the reign of the third Caliph Hazrat Usman, the most rigorous scrutiny of the texts was carried out. A commission of Quranic experts checked all the texts that were in existence and discarded inconsistencies. A joint agreement of the commission was necessary before anything was removed.[86] The result was a copy so thoroughly cross checked that chances of error were almost down to zero. The confirmed copies were then sent to different parts of the Muslim world. Since the scripture had undergone such intense scrutiny, the Qurans that are being read today are identical to the oldest documents in existence today.

The Hadeeth

After the Quran, the second religious text of Islam is the "Hadeeth." The word Hadeeth means an "account" or a "report". In the initial days of Islam, the Muslim community relied heavily on the words and actions of their Prophet for guidance in social, political, and economic matters. After his death, his words and actions had to be preserved for the future generations. Since oral traditions had no permanence, Islamic scholars compiled a series of literature called "Hadeeth" or "accounts." These were words and actions of the Prophet as remembered by his companions.

---

[86] Bucaille, p. 130

The scrutiny and compiling of the Hadeeth did not start until a century after the Prophet's death. Thus, in order to separate genuine oral accounts from false or exaggerated ones, scholars of that time developed a system called "Isnad". For every account regarding the life of the Prophet, scholars traced a chain of transmitters that went back almost three generations. Even if there was one person in that chain of transmission whose credibility was in question, the whole account was discarded as weak. Based on this method, volumes of work were produced in such great detail that minor information such as how many times the Prophet brushed his teeth was also recorded.

The first collection of accounts was compiled by Malik ibn Anas. Later on, many other works were produced with Sahih (authentics) of Bukhari and Muslim being the most authoritative ones. The rest were those of Abu Dawood, Tirmidhi, anNasa, and Ibn Maja.

Mystery of the Islamic Scriptures

Let us imagine a situation for a moment. Let's say that an archeological site is being dug. The team of archeologists working on the project suddenly discovers an old scripture dating back almost fourteen centuries. As they go through this ancient writing, they discover the fourteen-century-old document contains scientific information that we have discovered only recently. Imagine what a stir this new discovery will cause in academic circles. History books would have to be re-written, television channels will be giving it full coverage, and newspapers' headlines will state that an ancient scripture contains facts of science that we've only discovered during the last century.

Now guess what? That has already been done! Right now at this very moment, there exists a book fourteen centuries old that not only contains things we have only recently discovered, but also things that are too advanced for today's minds (such as UFOs and their origin). Unfortunately, it never got the press and television coverage, nor has it been given its legitimate place in academic circles.

Maurice Bucaille was a medical doctor with an interest in religions. In order to study the Quran, Bucaille learned Arabic and did a thorough study of the scripture. He was stunned to see that this book, recorded in the sixth century A.D., contained modern scientific information that was only unearthed a few years ago. He then turned to investigate the authenticity of the scripture, and then finally published the results of his findings in a book called *The Bible, The Quran, and Science*. This book was definitely one of the most influential books written on Islam.

For instance, Bucaille pointed to the "Big Bang" theory that the universe resulted from a cosmic explosion. The entire cosmos was joined together when a giant explosion occurred, and the physical universe came into existence. He also pointed out that the Big Bang is an ongoing explosion and that is why the universe is constantly expanding at a very fast pace. He then made a reference to the following verse of the Quran:

> "Do not the unbelievers see that the heavens and the earth were joined together before we *split them apart?* And we created life from water so will they not then believe?" (Quran 21:30)

This passage to Bucaille was a clear reference to the Big Bang. The mention of life originating from water is also seen as scientifically accurate. Furthermore, the Quran goes on to mention the expansion of the universe:

"And We created the heavens with *force*; and, verily, it is We who are steadily *expanding* it." (Al Quran 51/47)

Life in plants was discovered in the year 1902 by an Indian scientist, Dr. Jagdesh Chandra Bose. After performing a series of experiments on plants, Dr. Bose published his findings in a book called *The Reaction of Living and Non Living*.

Almost fourteen hundred years before Dr. Bose came out with his discovery, the Quran had mentioned "pairs" (male and female) in the animal kingdom.

"God is the one who sent water down from the skies and thereby brought forth pairs of plants each separate from the other." (20:53)

Bucaille's research caused a stir in religious circles both in the East and in the West. Muslim groups were now propagating Islam as a scientifically-backed religion, and Christians were trying to develop a counter argument. Critics remained skeptical, maintaining that theorists like Bucaille were chopping off the edges of scientific research to fit into the Quran. The fiercest argument against Bucaille came not from the Christian West, but from a Pakistani scientist, Dr. Pervez Hoodbhoy.

"Bucaille's method is simple. He asks his readers to ponder on some Quranic verse and then, from a variety of meanings that could be assigned to the verse, he pulls out the one which is consistent with some scientific fact."

In the midst of this discourse, came Dr. Keith L. Moore, an associate professor of anatomy and dean of basic sciences at the

University of Toronto. Professor Moore studied the Quran and was surprised to see that passages of the scripture contained detailed information about the development of the embryo into the fetus. Such information could not have existed during the time that the Quran was compiled.

> "He makes you in the wombs of your mothers in stages, one after another, in three veils of darkness." *Sura 39:6.*

Dr. Moore pointed out that although we do not know what human beings underwent during development in the uterus (womb), the first known illustration in the uterus was drawn in the fifteenth century by Leonardo da Vinci. It was only after the seventeenth century that the microscope was invented, and the stages of human embryo were not realized until the twentieth century.

Professor Moore was convinced that the three veils that were being described were (1) the anterior abdominal wall, (2) the uterine wall, and (3) the amniochorionic membrane.

The Quran then goes on to explain:

> "Then we placed him as a drop in a place of rest." (23:13)

Traditionally, the "drop" had been interpreted as the sperm drop, but Moore stated that this was in fact the zygote which is kept in a uterus (a place of rest) after being divided to form the blastocyst. In another passage, the Quran mentions the drop as a "mixed drop"; a description that applies more to the zygote which is a mixture of sperm and ovum.

> "Then we made the drop into a leech-like structure." (23:14)

The Arabic word "Alaqa" means a leech or a bloodsucker. This appears to be the perfect description for an embryo between days 7–24. It is during this time that the embryo clings to the endometrium of the uterus in the same way a leech clings to the skin. It also derives blood from the deciduas just like a leech derives blood from its host.

Dr. Moore went on to say, "It is remarkable how much the embryo of 23-24 days resembles a leech. As there were no microscopes or lenses available in the seventh century, doctors would not have known that the human embryo had this leech-like appearance."[87]

"Then of that leech-like structure, We made a chewed lump."
(Al Quran 23:14)

According to Dr. Moore, the embryo's chewed-like appearance, which appears during the end of the fourth week, comes from somites which resemble teeth marks.

"Then We made out of the chewed lump, bones, and clothed the bones in flesh." (23:14)

The next stage is the development of cartilage, which later turns into bone. Then muscle (flesh) develops around them.

"Then We developed out of it another creature." (23:14)

Dr. Moore's paper, which was published in *The Journal of the Islamic Medical Association 3* added more weight to the Bucaille argument of the Quran foretelling modern science.

We know that concepts like the Big Bang and embryology were unexplained mysteries for people of sixth century. Why would the Quran contain them? The only reason could be that the book is not addressing a particular generation at a particular time in history; instead it is addressing the entire humanity as a collective whole. If that is the case, then wouldn't the same book contain references to phenomenon we consider "unexplained" in our time?

CHAPTER 6

FLYING SAUCERS OF IBLEES

Mention of Extraterrestrial Visitors in the Quran and Hadeeth

Let's just admit it. It is not a comforting thought that we have been visited by extraterrestrials. For most people, it is frightening to know that their space has been violated by extraterrestrial intruders who have the ability to come and go undetected, and that they have taken human beings with them (most of the time against their wishes), performed medical experiments on them, and have been cross breeding with them. It is even more uncomfortable to know that the organizations that we put our trust in to provide us with security—governments, military, and law enforcement agencies—have not been able to do much to protect citizens in this situation. The whole hierarchal order, in which we put our sense of security, gets questioned if the thought of extraterrestrial contact is acknowledged.

Denying the phenomenon, on the other hand, gives a sense of relief, a sense of security, and, most of all, it restores our confidence in the world order and the institutions that we trust to look after us. The natural psychological response in this situation is to deny the very existence of alien contact in almost every possible way. We can deny it by giving counter-explanations of various sorts. These counter-explanations serve as psychological "rat-holes" for the human race to hide in. They reassure us of our already existing world view. There are many different psychological rat holes available to the modern individual. "All UFOs are hoaxes!" is one rat hole. "All UFOs are experimental military aircrafts!" is another rat hole, and there are whole series of psychological rat holes that one can withdraw in when confronted with the UFO phenomenon.

For Muslims, there is one very big psychological rat hole and that is the religion rat hole. Muslims see their religion as an all explaining, complete way of looking at the world and if anything is not part of their religious belief system, it doesn't exist. The people in the Muslim world, who have taken the UFO phenomenon seriously, are very few compared to those in the West. Most of the Muslims are not well informed about the subject in the first place to form any opinion either for or against. Those who are aware of the phenomenon are hiding in their all-secure "religion rat hole," which, in their opinion, assures them that they are "Ashraf-ul-Makhlooqaat," that is, the "preferred" creation of God.

To most Muslims, it would come as a great shock to know that the very rat hole in which they are hiding confirms the recent findings of modern UFOology. Everything that they have been reading in this book has been in their religious texts for centuries. What if Muslims, who are 25 percent of the world's population, were to all of a sudden, discover that in order to be Muslims they must believe in UFOs for their Prophet has mentioned them and the Quran confirms their existence.

Before we begin to examine Quranic verses and passages from the recorded Hadeeth (traditions of Prophet Muhammad), I must once again remind the reader that the Quran is different from other religious scriptures in the sense that it claims to be the very word of God. In other words, according to the scriptures' own claim, it is not the word of a human being telling what the Prophet had said; it isn't even the word of the Prophet saying what God told him, but the very word of God himself written in the first person.

Plurality of "Words" in the Quran

Throughout the text of the Quran, we find that the author (God) refers to himself as "Rab-ul-Aalameen," which means "Lord of the Worlds." This "plurality" of the worlds has been emphasized time and time again in different verses, in different chapters, and at different times.

"Verily, this is the revelation from the Lord of the *Worlds*."

(Al-Quran, 26:192)

"This is no less than a Message to (all) the *Worlds*."

(Al-Quran, 38:87)

"And the unbelievers would almost trip thee (Muhammad) up with their eyes when they hear the Message; and they say: "Surely he is possessed! But it (the Quran) is nothing less than a Message to all the worlds."

(Al-Quran, 68:51-52)

Furthermore, as we read through the Quran, we see that the scripture addresses two separate worlds, the world of humans and the world of "Jinns".

"Soon We shall settle your affairs O' *both ye Worlds.*"

(Al-Quran, 55.31)

What exactly does the Quran mean by world of the Jinns? Passages from the Quran and Hadeeth (recorded traditions of Prophet Muhammad) give us very detailed information about the Jinns and their origin.

Islam, from its very beginning, has recognized the existence of three separate species of beings. The first ones are angels or "Malaik." These are known to be beings created out of light. The second ones are humans, and the third ones are Jinns. While investigating the UFO phenomenon, it is this third type that should hold our interest. Even though Islam has never officially disputed the existence of Jinn, Muslim scholars, upon not finding any rational explanation to back up the concept, have shoved the subject into the realm of the "spiritual world." This tends to imply that no rational explanation can be given of these beings, nor is one needed. It is because of this attitude that, for fourteen hundred years, very little investigative work has been done on the subject. Today, even though Muslims, who form a quarter of the world's population, believe in Jinns, their understanding of the Jinn is shaped more by cultural folklore than by any investigative research. The only recent investigative work done on this subject that I am aware of is the PhD thesis of Bilal Phillips, who approached the subject of the Jinns from demonic possession's point of view.

When analyzed in the light of modern UFOology, these centuries old passages from the Quran and Hadeeth will take the ground from under the feet of most UFO researchers. The literal meaning of the word "Jinn" is to conceal one's presence or to hide from observation. Indeed, from the UFO behavior we have gone over in the previous sections of this book, this title seems to confirm the phenomenon we have been talking about. An entire chapter in the Quran is named after these beings that travel through the skies at lightning speeds and have the ability to teleport objects by materializing and de-materializing them. In "Surah Jinn" (Chapter of the Jinns, in the Quran), we find that these beings were present in the skies of Mecca when the verses of the Quran were being revealed to Prophet Muhammad on Mount Hira. They listened to the revelation from a high position and then returned to their cosmic origins to inform their people. This is mentioned very clearly in the following verse:

"Say: It has been revealed to me that a company of Jinns listened (to the Qur'an). They said, 'We have really heard a wonderful Recital!'"

(Al-Quran, 72:01)

"And when We inclined toward thee (Muhammad) certain of the jinn, who wished to hear the Qur'an and when they were in its presence, said: 'Give ear!' and when it was finished, turned back to their people, warning."

(Al-Quran, 46:29)

Their ability to travel in space is clearly documented as well.

"And we (the jinns) sought to *reach the heavens* but found it filled with strong guards and flaming stars."

(Al-Quran, 72:08)

"We (the Jinns) used, indeed to sit there in *(hidden) stations* to (steal) a hearing; but any who listens now will find a flaming fire waiting for him in ambush."

(Al-Quran, 72:09)

Exactly the same verse has been translated by Pickthal, which is another translator of the Quran, and is as follows:

"And we used to sit on *places (high)* therin to listen. But he who listeneth now will find a flame in wait for him."

"Hidden stations" in the sky? "Places high?" Are these verses talking about the same mysterious flying machines that appear and disappear on modern radars, and have played hide and seek with the human race for centuries?

"And we (jinns) know that we can not escape Allah on Earth, nor can we escape him through *flight.*"

(Al-Quran, 72:12)

Notice the word "flight" at the end of the verse.

Prophet Solomon's Alien Alliance

Modern UFO reports are full of incidents in which human beings, as well as large objects as big as automobiles, have been "teleported" by UFOs. The Jinn's ability to teleport things is also stated in the Quran. The Quran tells us that King Solomon, (who is a Prophet in Islam as well as in Judaism and Christianity) was in alliance with these space visitors. He used their gravity neutralizing ability to construct huge temples to the worship of one God. Furthermore, on one occasion, he surprised Queen Sheba (Queen Saba as she is mentioned in the Quran) by using these beings to "teleport" her throne into his palace. These are the passages that talk about this event:

> "He said (to his own men): 'Ye chiefs! which of you can bring me her throne before they come to me in submission?" Said an 'Ifrit, of the Jinns: "I will bring it to thee before thou rise from thy council: indeed I have full strength for the purpose, and may be trusted." Said one who had knowledge of the Book: "I will bring it to thee within the twinkling of an eye!" Then when (Solomon) saw it placed firmly before him, he said: "This is by the Grace of my Lord!- to test me whether I am grateful or ungrateful! and if any is grateful, truly his gratitude is (a gain) for his own soul; but if any is ungrateful, truly my Lord is Free of all Needs, Supreme in Honour ! He said: "Transform her throne out of all recognition by her: let us see whether she is guided (to the truth) or is one of those who receive no guidance." So when she arrived, she was asked, "Is this thy throne?" She said, "It was just like this; and knowledge was bestowed on us in advance of this, and we have submitted to Allah (in Islam)". And he diverted her from the worship of others besides Allah: for she was (sprung) of a people that had no faith".
>
> (Al-Quran, 27:39-43)

> "*(We gave him) certain of the jinn, who worked before him by permission of his Lord.* And such of them as deviated from Our command, them We caused to taste the punishment of flaming Fire."
>
> (Al Quran, 34:12)

The Sky Gods of pre-Islamic Arabia

Another thing to be noted in Islamic scriptures is the mention of alien worship in pre-Islamic Arabia. Archeological UFOology has asserted that ancient civilizations worshipped visitors from space. Rock paintings of flying saucers and astronauts have been found on walls of ancient temples dedicated to the worship of these "sky gods." According to the Quran, pagan Arabs of pre-Islamic Arabia worshipped the Jinns before the dawn of Islam. Consider this verse from the Quran:

> "And on the day when He (God) will gather them all together, He will say unto the angels: Did these worship you? They will say: Be Thou Glorified. Thou (alone) art our Guardian, not them! Nay, but *they worshipped the jinn*; most of them were believers in them."
>
> (Al-Quran, 34: 40,41)[88]

Alien worship among the pagans was a practice very well documented in the Hadeeth (recorded traditions of Prophet Muhammad) as well.

> "Abdullah b. Mas'ud reported in connection with the words of Allah, the Exalted and Glorious: 'Those to whom they call upon, themselves seek the means or access to their Lord as to whoever of them becomes nearest' (xvii. 57) that it related to *a party of Jinn who were being worshipped and they embraced Islam*, but those who worshipped them kept on worshipping them (though the Jinn whom the misguided people worshipped had become Muslims). It was then that this verse was revealed."
>
> (Sahih Muslim, Book 43: Number 7182)

Von Daniken, a Swiss archeologist, wrote his famous but controversial book *Chariots of the Gods*. His book provided

---

[88] Translated by Pickthal

convincing evidence that what many ancient religions worshipped as "sky gods" were in reality visitors from space. Von Daniken from that point on became the father of the "astronaut god" theory. His research raised a very important question. "Is God an alien?" He also argued that the Biblical cities of Sodom and Gomorah, which according to the Bible were destroyed by the wrath of God, were in reality destroyed by an alien race that used a nuclear bomb for the purpose. The event is mentioned in the Quran as well and **is** therefore as important to Islam as it is to Christianity or Judaism.

An important point to be noted in the Quran is that this scripture, which was recorded in the sixth century, answered the fundamental question Von Daniken would pose thirteen centuries later. "Is "God" or "Allah" or "Jehovah" an alien?"

> "And they imagine kinship between Him (God) and the Jinns: but the Jinns know well that they will be brought before (Him)."
>
> (Al- Quran, 37:158)[89]

> "Say: If the whole of mankind and Jinns were to gather together to produce the like of this Quran, they could not produce the like thereof, even if they backed up each other with help and support."
>
> (Al- Quran, 17:88)

Was Prophet Muhammad on Board a UFO?

Islamic scriptures have also confirmed the possibility of abduction cases as Islamic texts state very clearly that Jinns have the

---

[89] Translated by Pickthal

ability to snatch human beings. In fact, the Prophet himself was taken away by them. According to the recorded traditions, the Prophet had at least two encounters with these space beings, which according to Professor Allen J. Hyenek's classification system, would be classified as CE-4s; that is, Close Encounters of the Fourth Kind.

In the first encounter, the Prophet was taken away by a group of Jinns. He was reported missing for a day and his companions searched for him. He was found the other day coming from a hill, and when they asked him the reason for his mysterious disappearance, he told them that Jinns had come to them seeking knowledge of the revelation (Islam). The Prophet went with them and gave them the scripture. Later, he was dropped by these beings on a hill top. The Prophet then took his companions and showed them the marks left by the burning engines of the spacecraft. This incident is recorded in the Hadeeth as "The Night of the Jinns."

> "Dawud reported from 'Amir who said: 'I asked 'Alqama if Ibn Mas'ud was present with the Messenger of Allah (may peace be upon him) on the night of the Jinn (the night when the Holy Prophet met them). He (Ibn Mas'uad) said: No, but we were in the company of the Messenger of Allah (may peace be upon him) one night and we missed him. We searched for him in the valleys and the hills and said. H*e has either been taken away (by jinn)* or has been secretly killed.' He (the narrator) said. 'We spent the worst night which people could ever spend. When it was dawn we saw him coming from the side of Hiri'.' He (the narrator) reported. We said: 'Messenger of Allah, we missed you and searched for you, but we could not find you and we spent the worst night which people could ever spend.' He (the Holy Prophet) said: *'There came to me an inviter on behalf of the Jinn* and I went along with him and recited

to them the Qur'an.' He (the narrator) said: 'He then went along with us and showed us *their traces and traces of their fires."*

(Sahih Muslim Book 004, Number 0903)

In December 1999, I had the opportunity to visit the site from where the Prophet was reportedly taken by the Jinns. In order to mark the place as a historic site, early Muslims constructed a mosque which was called "Masjid-al-Jinn" (Mosque of the Jinns). In the centuries that followed, the mosque underwent many renovations. Today, Mecca city has spread so far that this site now lies in the heart of the city. Saudi government had cordoned off the area for a new renovation when I was there in 1999.

The second encounter was a failed abduction attempt at the life of Prophet Muhammad. There are many modern day abductions where abductees claim to have been hit by a beam of light. The light paralyzes the individual and he is taken into the UFO by humanoid beings. Prophet Muhammad also reports a similar kind of abduction attempt. It is reported that he was praying when his prayers were interrupted by a Jinn, who tried to "burn his face with a light". Witnesses that were present on the occasion reported having seen the Prophet physically struggling with an invisible man. The Prophet was seen extending out a hand as if he was struggling with something. When asked, the Prophet responded that a Jinn called "Iblees"[90] tried

---

[90] The word Iblees is used in the Quran to refer to a particular Jinn. Sometimes the word is also used to refer to his followers, a particular 'tribe' among the Jinns. The tribe of 'Iblees.' A detailed discussion on the subject will follow in the latter part of the chapter.

to interrupt his prayers, and he physically overpowered the creature. The Prophet said that he choked the humanoid to the point where he could feel the cold saliva of the being on his hands.[91] This is how the event has been reported in the Hadeeth:

> Abu Darda' reported: Allah's Messenger (may peace be upon him) stood up (to pray) and we heard him say: "I seek refuge in Allah from thee." Then said:" curse thee with Allah's curse" three times, then he stretched out his hand as though he was taking hold of something. When he finished the prayer, we said: Messenger of Allah, we heard you say something during the prayer which we have not heard you say before, and we saw you stretch out your hand. He replied: Allah's enemy Iblees came with a flame of fire to put it in my face, so I said three times:" I Seek refuge in Allah from thee." Then I said three times:" I curse thee with Allah's full curse." But he did not retreat (on any one of these) three occasions. Thereafter I meant to seize him. I swear by Allah that had it not been for the supplication of my brother, Sulaiman, he would have been bound, and made an object of sport for the children of Medina.
>
> (Sahih Muslim Book 4, Number 1106)

When a twelve-hundred-year-old account describes an alien encounter, it can't possibly use words such as UFOs, aliens, or stun beam. After analyzing a great number of abduction accounts, I am convinced that when the Prophet says that the being (referred to as Iblees), tried to "burn his face with a flame of fire," he is talking about the same stun beam that abductees describe in modern cases of alien abduction.

---

[91] Reported by Aamir ibn Abdullah ibn Masood on the authority of his father and collected by Imam Ahmad.

Alien Abductions during the Time of Prophet Muhammad

During Prophet Muhammad's time, it can be assumed that abductions were taking place on a massive scale, for the Prophet repeatedly warned his followers to protect themselves against being taken away by these creatures. One reported tradition the Prophet stated:

> "Cover your utensils and tie your water skins, and close your doors and keep your children close to you at night, as the Jinns spread out at such time and snatch things away."
>
> (Sahih Bukhari, Vol. 4, Book 54, Number 533)

Another tradition records:

> Allah's Apostle said, "When night falls (or when it is evening), stop your children from going out, for the 'Shayateen' spread out at that time. But when an hour of the night has passed, release them and close the doors and mention Allah's Name, for Shaitan does not open a closed door. Tie the mouth of your water skin and mention Allah's Name; cover your containers and utensils and mention Allah's Name. Cover them even by placing something across it, and extinguish your lamps."
>
> (Sahih Bukhari, Vol. 7, Book 69, Number 527)

Tribe of Iblees! Its Alien Origin

One thing that needs to be noted in the last few traditions is the use of the words "Iblees" and "Shaitan" to refer to what we are beginning to recognize as extraterrestrial life forms. The word Shaitan in Arabic simply means "Satan." "Iblees," according to Islamic beliefs, is a tribe of Jinns named after their great ancestor whose story is an interesting one. Christians and Jews will see many familiarities in this.

The Jinns, according to the Quran, have existed long before we humans appeared as a species. It is stated that the Jinns were created from fire or flame.

> "And the Jinn race we had created before, from the fire of a scorching wind."
>
> (Al- Quran, 15:27)

The same verse has been translated by two other translators, Phickthal and Shakir as:

> "And the Jinn we create aforetime *of essential fire.*"
>
> (As translated by Pickthal)

> "And the jinns we created before *from intensely hot fire.*" .
>
> (As translated by Shakir)

Muslims believe that Iblees was a Jinn who was a very devoted worshipper of God before human kind was created. When God created the human race, he created Adam and breathed his own spirit into him. All of the creation was then asked to lie prostrate to Adam for he was given the title of "Ashraf-ul-Makhlooqaat," the exalted or the preferred creation of God. All the creation prostrated except Iblees who claimed to be a superior creation over Adam. Because of his disobedience, his special status was taken away and he was declared Shaytaan or "Satan." He then requested respite till the day they (i.e., humans) were raised up. God gave him respite.

So far, there is nothing in the field of modern UFOlogy that would confirm the above mentioned incident, for if it happened it must have happened millions of years ago. But assuming that the above mentioned story also has some UFO-related reality to it just like the other verses we have examined, the descendents of Iblees would have multiplied just like the descendents of Adam since then. It is these that the Quran refers to as "the tribe of Iblees" or the Shayateen (devils).

> "He (i.e., Satan) and his tribe watch you from a position from where you can not see them."
>
> (Al-Quran, 7:27)

Alien Mothership or Throne of Iblees?

Thomas Roy Dutton, an aviation and astroengineer of British Aerospace, was interested in determining whether UFO sightings had any connection to the position of various planets. After investigating hundreds of UFO sightings, Dutton discovered an interesting pattern. Sightings took place all around the world in certain cycles with surprising regularity. He concluded that there were ten motherships stationed around the earth from which scout ships were sent out for short missions. These motherships, Dutton believed, would not rotate with the 24-hour rotation of the earth around it own axis. Instead, they would remain constant at a particular spot until they were exactly above the geographical area in which missions were to be carried out.[92]

In the sixth century A.D., around fourteen hundred years before Duttin carried out his investigations, Prophet Muhammad said that

---

[92] Hesseman, p. 97

Iblees set his throne on the sea from where he sends his troops to different areas of the world to tempt mankind. This saying was recorded by Imam Muslim in his Sahih, on the authority of Jabir. This is how he has narrated it:

> "Iblees sets his throne on water. From there he sends out his troops to tempt mankind. The one whom he regards closest to him is the one that causes the greatest temptation."
>
> (Sahih Muslim, Book 39, Number 6755)

Mutual UFO Network (MUFON) is the world's largest organization carrying out research into UFOs. Their field investigator's exam contains a section on animal reactions to UFO presence. It is reported through many documented CE-4 cases that animals become extremely agitated before a UFO sighting. Dogs begin to bark and farm animals start making noise. The exact animal reaction to UFOs is also documented in the sayings of Prophet Muhammad. It is reported in the Hadeeth that the Prophet said:

> "If you hear the barking of a dog or the braying of a donkey at night, seek refuge in Allah from Shaitaan (Satan), because they see what you do not."
>
> (Sunan Abu Dawood, Vol. 3, Number 5084)

Twenty-four-year-old Rose was awakened by the sound of dogs only to find out that her farm house near Nimes was visited by three aliens, whom she described as seven feet tall.[93] Along with these aliens was also a human being who told her that he was a teacher

---

[93] See details of this case in Chapter 3

who was visited by these space beings in the year 1932. He agreed to go along with them and they took him to their "far away world," where time passed much slower than Earth years. Physically, he looked in his late 20s, but in Earth years he was forty-five. The slow passage of time in the alien world had made him age slower than that of the humans.

Incidents like these may sound like pure science fiction, but the Quran very clearly confirms them.

> "True there were persons among mankind who took shelter with the persons among the Jinns, but they increased them in folly."
>
> (Al-Quran, 72:6)

Psychic Phenomenon! Its Satanic Origins

Rose's case was interesting from another perspective as well. After her meeting with these humanoid beings, she developed psychic abilities. Through psychic visions she began seeing things before they actually happened. She wasn't the only one. As explained in Chapter 4, a great number of people who have come in contact with these space visitors have mysteriously started receiving psychic visions.

Psychic phenomenon is another area of the paranormal that modern science has not been able to explain. Even though its overlap with the UFO experiences has recently been established, Hadeeth (recorded traditions of Prophet Muhammad) explained the phenomenon over twelve centuries ago.

> "Some people asked Allah's Apostle about the fore-tellers He said, 'They are nothing.' They said, 'O Allah's Apostle! Sometimes they tell us of a

thing which turns out to be true.' Allah's Apostle said, 'A *Jinn snatches that true word* and pours it into the ear of his friend. The foreteller then mixes with that word one hundred lies.'"

(Narrated By Aisha, Vol. 7, Book 71, Number 675)

The Prophet is further reported to have said that the news of the future, or "the news of the heavens" as it is referred to in many traditions, is the truth and "a Jinn snatches away and then cackles into the ear of ally as the hen does. And then they mix it with a hundred lies."[94] The Prophet had also added at a separate occasion, "If they (the Jinns) narrate only what they managed to snatch it would be correct, but they alloy it with lies and make additions to it."

It is because of this that psychic consultations have been frowned upon in Islam.

Safiyya reported from some of the wives of Allah's Apostle (may peace be upon him) Allah's Apostle (may peace be upon him) having said: "He who visits a diviner ('Arraf) and asks him about anything, his prayers extending to forty nights will not be accepted."

(Sahih Muslim, Book 26, Number 5540)

Spirits of the Planets

Ahmed Ibn Tamiyah, a famous scholar, wrote *Majmoo-al-Fatwa*, a collection of Islamic rulings on various issues explaining the relationship of devil worshippers to the sky gods that they worshipped. It is interesting to note that these devil worshippers used the term "spirits of the planets" to refer to their sky gods.

---

[94] Reported by Urwa, Book 26, Number 5536

"People of misguidance and heresies, those who are ascetic and worshippers but not according to the Shariah, sometimes have a strong influence that draws many to the places of Satan in which it is prohibited to pray. This is because the devils descend upon them and the devils talk to them about some matters the same way they talk to fortune tellers. In the same manner, they enter the statues and idols and talk to the worshippers of the idols. They help them in some of their needs in the same manner they help magicians. In the same manner, they help the worshipper of idols, the sun, the moon and the planets when they worship them in the manner they think that are deserving of, of sanctifying them, to dressing and lighting incense for them and so on. Devils, that they call '*spirits of the planets*', descend upon them and meet some of their needs."[95]

Phantom Pregnancies in Islamic Shariah Law

UFOologists who investigate abductions find themselves dealing with a number of cases in which the abductees report being impregnated by their alien abductors. These "sexual encounters" are not uncommon. The explanation most commonly given is that aliens seem to be fascinated with our genetic makeup, and therefore have tried to cross breed with us. The purpose of these sexual encounters, therefore, is to produce "half-breeds"—species that are half-human and half-alien. Selected cases out of these sexual abductions are discussed in Chapter 4 "Raped by Aliens."

---

[95] Ahmed Ibn Tamiyah, Majmoo ul Fatwa, Volume 19, p. 41

It has always been a problem for Islamic scholars to explain the concept of Jinns having sexual relations with humans. Such cases are reported in Islamic traditions. First of all, the very existence of the Jinn has remained a theoretical problem for Muslim scholars because their scriptures were talking about a concept too advanced for their time. When the issue was shoved into the realm of the "spiritual world," Muslim scholars conveniently explained the Jinns as spiritual beings. Another problem emerged with this interpretation of the Jinn. This problem was the inability to explain sexual encounters between humans and Jinn. As we studied earlier, there have been space visitors who took Prophet Muhammad with them and converted to Islam after receiving the revelation. A theoretical problem that came much later after the death of the Prophet was whether sexual relationships with these beings, and marriages with them, were permissible under "Sharia," the Islamic Law.

Ali-ibn-Muhammad was born in 974 A.D. in Basrah and transferred to Baghdad later. Commonly known as Abu-Hasan-al-Maawardee, he was a scholar of Islamic law and the Chief Judge during the time of Abassid Caliph al-Qaim-bin-Amrillah. He was a leading authority on Islamic Law and a prolific writer who had produced works such as *Aadab-ad-Duniya-wad-Deen, Al-ahkaam-al-Sultaniya, and Aalam-an-Nabuwah*. When asked about the Islamic ruling concerning humans having sexual relations and marriages with the Jinns, he rejected the possibility altogether. "The intellect rejects (the possibility of sex between human and Jinn) due to the differences in their species, natures, and senses," he had stated. "Man is corporeal and the Jinn are incorporeal. Man was created from clay, while the Jinn were created from fire. Thus, mixing would not be possible with such differences, and the offspring would be inconceivable."[96]

Other scholars, such as Sayootee and Ibn Tameeyah were convinced that sexual relationships have been going on between human beings and Jinns. Ibn Tameeyah wrote, "Jinns and humans may also have sexual intercourse with each other and beget children. This is a frequent occurrence that is well known to many."[97] The fact that he mentioned sexual relations between humans and Jinns as "frequent" means that these "sexual abductions" were a frequent occurrence at the time. Thus, not being fully aware of the nature of the phenomenon they were dealing with, Islamic scholars have debated this issue for centuries. There has been a two-fold debate: Whether a sexual relationship is possible between humans and Jinns. And, if possible, is it permissible under Islamic law? Since there was lack of scripture-based evidence to rule out such relationships as forbidden (*haram*), most scholars declared these relationships as disliked (*makrooh*).

It is reported that in seventh century A.D., some people in Yemen wrote a letter to a famous Islamic scholar and asked him about marriages with Jinns. The scholar, who was very well known at this time, accepted the possibility of the sexual union between the two species and responded by saying, "I do not see in it any religious objection, but I consider it detestable. For, if a woman found

---

[96] Al-Jaami-li-Aakham al-Quran, vol. 13, p. 211
[97] Majmoo-ul-Fatwa, vol. 19, p. 39

pregnant is asked, 'Who is your husband?' and she replies, 'He is one of the Jinns,' this would lead to much corruption in the principles in the religion of Islam." The scholar was no other than Imam Maalik-bin-Anas, compiler of the earliest collection of Hadeeth, "Al-Muwatta," and founder of one of the four schools of Islamic jurisprudence.[98]

I have tried to remain as objective as possible in my study of Jinns and UFOs. As we have seen, the similarity between the UFO phenomenon and Jinns from Islamic scriptures is too great to be ruled out as a mass coincidence. From the very meaning of the word "Jinn" to detailed events recorded in Islamic texts, everything that Islamic scriptures say about "Jinns" and "Shayateen" (plural of what the Christian West understands as Satan), fits recent UFO findings. Most religions have recognized the concept of the "devil," but used different names for it such as Lucifer, Satan, Iblees, Shaytaan, etc. If we can somehow see beyond this jargon of terms, we would soon realize that what these terms ultimately refer to is what we know today as the UFO phenomenon. This "Satan is an ALIEN!" idea is frightening for a religious-minded person, regardless of what religion he belongs to. The same idea is not any less frightening to the secular democracies in the Western world, for, after fighting very hard to separate religion from the state, they must come to terms with the fact that what they are dealing with, in the form of UFOs, is the devil himself.

---

[98] Majmoo ul Fatwa, vol. 19, p. 39

CHAPTER 7

History of Jinns

Alien Contact in Islamic History

It is reported that during the Caliphate of Hazrat Umer bin Al Khattab, a man went to pray the late night prayers (*Isha*) and never returned. His wife appeared before Umer and explained her situation. Umer instructed that she wait for four years for her husband, after which she would be permitted to marry another man. She waited for the appointed time and then got married. A few days after her second marriage, the disappeared husband returned and was presented before the Caliph. Upon inquiring, the man revealed that after he had left for his night prayers, he was abducted and imprisoned by a group of Jinn. He had spent a long time with his abductors living on things on which Gods name had not been announced and drinking from juices that had not turned to liquor. The Jinns who had abducted him were later attacked by another group of Jinn. A battle took place between the two groups and the attacking party overpowered his abductors. They then asked him about his religion and when he replied that he was a Muslim, they (victorious Jinns) told him that they followed the same religion and were therefore not permitted to keep him as a prisoner. They gave him the choice to either live with them or return to his home planet. He chose the latter and was thus freed. The Caliph, after listening to this story, gave the man the right to either take his wife back or divorce her so that she could live with her new husband.[99]

Islamic history is full of incidents like these. Visits by strange-looking creatures, people disappearing for extended periods of time and then reappearing, and humans bearing hybrid children that grew up to have mystical powers. A great number of sufi saints whose graves are being worshipped had also undergone similar experiences. Unfortunately, contemporary historians have paid little attention to these accounts ruling them out as nonsensical folklore not deserving any place in modern rational discourse.

While going through these accounts, we find a lot of cases that bear striking resemblance to cases of modern alien contact. Anyone who has done a serious study of UFO phenomenon will know that the remarkable details in these accounts could not be the product of anyone's imagination. But, then of course, we also find cases that seem to come more from human imagination than any actual physical or metaphysical experience. For example, Egyptologists have always wondered how ancient Egyptians cut the stones for the pyramids. What instruments were used to cut solid stones into such symmetrical, rectangular blocks?

---

[99] Suyooti, p. 193

In his work, *Fazail-e-Bait-ul-Muqaddas*, Abu Bakr Wasti narrates the tradition of how the Jinns cut the stone for the construction of Al Aqsa mosque. The traditions states that King Solomon wanted to build a mosque from stones that had not been cut by metal. He assembled the "shayateen" (devils) and said to them, "Allah has commanded that I build a house whose stone had not been cut by metal." The devils then replied that, "No one has the power to do this except a Jinn, who comes to drink water from a spot in the sea." He (Solomon) then told them to go and take the water from that place in the ocean and fill it with wine. When the Jinn came to drink water, he smelled the odor and did not drink. But when he got very thirsty and drank, that is how he was captured."

The same story goes on to tell how this captured Jinn asked Solomon for a steel pot so big that even a large group would not be able to lift it. He then asked that the pot be placed on small vultures. He went toward the pot, but was not able to reach the vulture. The vulture then flew away and when it returned, it carried in its beak a twig. He then placed the twig on the pot and the pot was cut into two. Hethen ran to pick up the twig, but the Jinn took it before he could reach it. This was used to make stone for Bait-ul-Muqqaddas.

Here we can see elements of folklore thrown in. We hear of Jinns drinking water from the ocean, part of ocean being emptied and filled with liquor, the Jinn getting drunk, etc. These are elements that bear no resemblance to modern UFO cases and are more likely to be figments of medieval imagination. While such historical accounts do give information that is useful, they cannot within themselves be treated as holistic truth. Without believing in the content of these stories, what we can safely conclude is that in the past, certain structures were built by an alien technology that was interpreted rather mystically by the people of that time.

A UFO Chased the Prophet during "Meraj"

Some time before his migration to Medina, the Prophet described an experience which came to be known as "Meraj," meaning the Ascent. This Meraj incident has been one of the most questioned episodes in Islamic history. According to traditions, the Prophet was awakened one night by the angel Gabriel, and taken into the skies on a beast described in recorded traditions as "Buraq." Details of this beast are still obscure and very little is recorded about it. Interestingly, the word Buraq means to shine or glitter with lightening.[100] According to Bukhari, it was smaller than a mule, bigger than an ass, and had wings.

Keeping in mind the aerodynamic description, the mention of wings, the shiny glittering surface, and lightning (which is most likely the jet wash from the afterburner), it seems more likely that this beast that took the Prophet in the skies was mechanical rather than biological. Since animals were the only mode of transportation that the people of that time were familiar with, it would be quite normal for them to interpret a small space vessel as a flying beast. The accounts go on to tell us that Buraq traveled through the air in flashes of speed with a rate of progression so fast that wherever its glance landed, in the next minute it was there.

---

[100] Cyril Glasse, p. 79

Mounted on this aerial vehicle, the Prophet went to Jerusalem where he met other Prophets including Abraham, Moses, and Jesus. He then led a prayer at the site of the Temple of Solomon. After its destruction by the Romans, the temple lay in ruins at that time. The Prophet then ascended to the skies to the divine presence. He described traveling through the seven heavens (symbolic of the degrees separating nonmanifestation from manifestations). Archangel Gabriel, who traveled with him, assumed his spiritual celestial form as they rose from one heaven to the other.

After experiencing a divine presence, he began his descent and as he was returning from Jerusalem to Mecca, the Prophet saw caravans traveling through the desert. The next morning when he shared this experience with people, the pagan tribes of Mecca, who had already declared him a lunatic, ridiculed him. Their mockery stopped when the caravans he had described finally arrived in the city confirming his statement.

Besides the aerodynamic description of "Buraq," this account of space travel through the universe is also important from another perspective. While the Prophet was taken into outer space, recorded traditions describe how he was pursued by a Jinn who followed him with a "burning flame." This is how the incident is mentioned in a Hadeeth:

It is narrated by Hazrat Yahya bin Saeed that when the Prophet was taken on the ascent (*Meraj*), he saw a very big Shaitan (Satan) pursuing him with a jet of flame. Whenever the Prophet looked at him, he was coming behind him. The Archangel Gabriel then said to the Prophet, "Should I not teach you the utterances that will cause his flame to blow out and leave him frustrated?" The Prophet

said, "Why not. Do teach me (the utterances)." Then Archangel
Gabriel asked the Prophet to repeat the following:

"I seek refuge in Allah's glory and position, through his (taught)
utterances, from the evil that descends from the skies or ascends
thereon. For no one amongst them can subjugate these utterances. And
from the evil of all that enters and leaves the earth, and from the
mischief makers of the day and the night. And from the stealers of the
night and of the day, except those who deliver good oh merciful."

We should pay attention to what is being said. Satan was
following the Prophet with a "jet of flame?" If people living in the
medieval age were to describe the afterburners of a spaceship, what
words would they use? Consider the lines of the utterances that
Gabriel gave to the Prophet. In his prayer, the Prophet was seeking
refuge from that which "descends from the skies and ascends
thereon," and that "which enters and leaves the earth?" How much
more accurate do the traditions have to be to explain that what is
being talked about here are alien space travelers?

Biologically Engineered Alien Viruses

AIDS is one of the most intriguing mysteries of this century. Its
origins are still under debate because no one knows for sure how it
came about. There is no vaccine and no cure. All we know is that it
has infected millions and continues to grow.

Most of us are familiar with the "AIDS-Conspiracy" theories that
are circulating through the internet and alternative literature. Many
have questioned the official AIDS story that the virus started in Africa
from chimpanzees and suddenly jumped species into humans. An al-

ternative theory is that AIDS is a form of biological warfare; a deliberately engineered (man-made) virus developed to depopulate the earth.

The purpose of my research is not to comment on the validity of these theories, but within the context of biological warfare I would like to bring into view certain traditions of the Prophet. According to the Hadeeth of the Prophet, certain viruses in the past were developed and planted by the Jinns to depopulate the earth. These passages from the Hadeeth relate to the plague, an epidemic that wiped out village after village during the Prophet's time.

> "Plague has an extremity that will reach my followers from their *enemies among the Jinn.* Its hump will be like the hump of a camel. Whoever stays in the lands infected by the plague will be like the soldier defending the frontiers of Islam, and the one who dies by it will achieve the status of a martyr, and the one who runs away from it will be like the one who runs away from the enemies of Islam in a battle field." [101]

The Prophet is obviously describing a disease that will be take human lives and will be from the Jinn. I am open to the possibility that what is being described is a biologically engineered alien virus.

Alien-Human Hybrids in Islamic History

Islamic History is filled with the mention of hybrid people that were half-human, half-Jinns. In one of his traditions, the Prophet mentioned a race of people that he called "Maghriboon."

---

[101] Sayooti, p. 198

Narrated by Aisha, Ummul Mu'minin:

"The Apostle of Allah said to me: 'Have the mugharribun been seen (or some other word) among you?' I asked: 'What do the mugharribun mean?' He replied: 'They are those in whom is a strain of the Jinn.'"[102]

Further explanation of these maghriboon comes from another tradition by Ibn Aseer Rahmallah.

"They are called "maghriboon" because another "fluid" (Arq) has been included in them or because they have been born by an outside race (*nasb*)."[103]

In a tradition relating to Hazrat Ali- ibn-Talib, the fourth Caliph of Islam and the cousin of the Prophet, mentions his meeting with a man whose mother claimed that he was the offspring of the Jinns. This is how the tradition reads:

"Hazrat Ali asked, 'Who knows this man?' One man from among those present stated, 'I know him. He is "Qaus" and his mother is also here.' So Hazrat Ali sent a messenger to his mother and asked her who his father was. She replied, 'I do not know. All I know is that during ignorance (pre-Islamic era), I was minding the sheep of my tribe when a thing with a shadowy face had intercourse with me from which I was impregnated, and that is how he was born.'"[104]

---

[102] Sunan Abu Dawood, Book 41, Number 5088
[103] Suyooti, p. 88
[104] Suyooti, p. 88

Abduction of Christ?

One of the concepts that separates Muslims from Christians is the Islamic concept that Jesus was "lifted up" by God, and will return before the apocalypse to bring peace into a war-torn world. The process of Jesus being "lifted up" has neither been explained nor been investigated by Muslim scholars. Since the prevailing religious mentality dictates that everything is possible by God, such investigations are considered useless.

The Quranic verses that mention Jesus not dying and being "raised" are as follows:

004.157. That they said (in boast), "We killed Christ *Jesus* the son of Mary, the Apostle of God"; but they killed him not, nor crucified him, but so it was made to appear to them, and those who differ therein are full of doubts, with no (certain) knowledge, but only conjecture to follow, for of a surety they killed him not.

004.158. Nay, God raised him up unto Himself; and God is exalted in power, wise;-

Though the return of Jesus is not mentioned anywhere in the Quran, there is a certain Hadeeth (tradition of the Prophet) that states that:

Abu Hureira reported that the Prophet (may peace be upon him) saying: There is no Prophet between me and him; that is, Jesus (may peace be upon him). He will descend (to the earth). When you see him, recognize him: a man of medium height, reddish fair, wearing two, light-yellow garments, looking as if drops were falling down from his head, though it will not be wet. He will fight for the people for the cause of Islam. He will break the cross, kill swine, and abolish jizyah. Allah will perish all religions except Islam. He will destroy the antichrist and will live on the earth for forty years, and then he will die. The Muslims will pray over him.[105]

Among Muslims those who are willing to believe without questioning do not find such traditions problematic. The short answer that everything is within the power of God is sufficient for them. It is only the religious skeptic and the critical thinker who is disturbed by them. He is forced to think how is it possible for a man to vanish from the face of the earth two thousand years ago and then return in the future and bring political upheaval? Are these traditions mere fabrications or are they talking about certain astrophysics that are yet to be discovered?

It has been stated that spacecrafts of the future will be equipped with photon propulsion systems. Theoretically, a rocket equipped with photon propulsion can reach 99 percent of the speed of light. According to Einstein's theory of relativity, time on board a spaceship traveling barely below light speed will in reality pass more slowly than on Earth. At 99 percent of the speed of light, 14.1 years of time on board our space vessel would be 100 years of time on Earth. So when our astronauts return back to Earth, a century would have been passed, yet they would only be fourteen years older.

Thus, what Islamic traditions regarding Jesus describe is not impossible within known laws of physics; the only prerequisite is

---

[105] Velinankode, pp. 343-344

space travel. Human beings could not space travel two thousand years ago. Then who could have done that? Was Jesus taken into the skies by the technologically advanced visitors? We know that UFO phenomenon has been going on thousands of years, and we know that in modern cases of alien contact people have been taken into outer space; so why should it be ruled out as an impossibility for Jesus? The readers should recall the 1952 Mary Rose case in which she met a school teacher who claimed to have been taken from Earth in 1932. Though he was forty-five by Earth years, he was physically in his 20s.[106]

UFOs Over Daghestan

In the early eighteenth century, an alien contact occurred over the hills of Daghestan (present day Chechnya) and this time the contactee was the militant and freedom fighter, Imam Shamyl of Daghestan.

British writer Lesley Blanch went into great detail to document the history of Imam Shamyl. In his biography of Shamyl, *The Sabres of Paradise*, he mentions his alien contact. Of course, while writing *The Sabres of Paradise Blanch*, he did not realize that what he was documenting was a Close Encounter of the Fourth Kind. Anyone with a little knowledge of UFO contact would have been able to spot the similarities right away.

While describing the childhood of Shamyl, Blanch writes, "The younger boy lived in the world of legends, peopled by mythological creatures, djinns and fabled monsters, which in his imagination

---

[106] Chapter 2, pg ***

inhabited a nearby plateau set among the desolate rock wastes, a region feared through out Daghestan. No villages would venture near after dusk: but the young Shamyl was in the habbites of spending the whole nights there, sharing said the villagers, some kind of sinister secret with the djinns, almas and peris whose Walpurgis Nacht revels were lit by *jets of flame which could be seen from afar, blazing up into the sky, curiously livid flames, flickering, falling and blazing up again.*"

Jets of flame that could be seen from afar? Blazing up into the sky, curiously livid flames, flickering, falling and blazing up again? Is it not strikingly similar to the known UFO behavior we have studied in previous chapters?

Imam Shamyl grew up to become a Muslim guerilla leader. He began to preach resistance against the Czars of Russia. In the following years, he, along with his "Murids," fought a series of bloody wars against the Czar's armies. Finally, after his last stand at Gounib, he was captured and imprisoned. In 1869, Shamyl was allowed to make his pilgrimage to Mecca where he drew large crowds. His name had become a legend throughout the Muslim lands and remains so even today; yet his "extraterrestrial" connections have never been realized.

The Prophet's Preventions against Alien Abduction

Alien abductions are a global phenomenon. UFO researchers and sociologists have worked laboriously to find a defense that would somehow protect people from being taken away. In some cases, even video cameras have been installed in the houses of the abductees to give them a sense of assurance that the abduction will not happen while they are being taped. Yet, since the presence of UFOs interferes with electronic devices, such methods have not worked very well.

In this section of the book, I would like to share with the readers certain "utterances" that were used by the Prophet for protection against the Jinn. Early Muslims believed that these prevented them from the alien's contact. They often memorized them while traveling through isolated regions. I do not have any recent case of these being used as preventions against alien contact, but Islamic history documents many cases in which people were protected by them. One example of a man being protected from abduction comes from a tradition by Hazrat Abdullah bin Masoud:

> It has been narrated by Hazrat Abdullah bin Masoud that from the people of Ahle-safa, everyone was invited to someone's house for dinner except me. I had not been invited by anyone. I was sitting in a mosque when the Prophet came. In his hands he held a date palm stick. He tapped it on my chest and asked me to come with him. Then he went away and I also went with him till we reached Baqi-Gharfaz. The Prophet then made a mark (on the ground) with his stick and said "Sit within this and stay here until I return." Then he walked away. I continued to watch him through the date palms until everything was covered in a dark mist and there was no contact left between us. I heard the sound of the Prophets stick and him saying, "Sit down." Finally, the dawn broke, the mist disappeared, and they also left. The Prophet then approached me and said, "If you had left this circle after my instructions, anyone from among these (Jinns) would have snatched

you away. Did you see anything?" I replied, "I saw some dark figures surrounded by a misty, white covering."[107]

One prayer that has been used by Muslims for protection against contact with the Jinn is the passage from the Quran, "Ayat-al-Kursi." The small verse that appears in the Surah Baqara has astronomical information in it. Below is the verse as uttered along with its English translation.

ALLAH-HO-LA ILAHA, ILA HUA AL HAIY-UL-QAYOOM

God! There is no god but He,-the Living, the Self-subsisting, Eternal.

LA TA KHIZOO SINA TANW-WALA NAOM

No slumber can seize Him nor sleep.

LAHOO MAFIZ SAMAWAT-E-WAMA-FIL-ARDH

His are all things in the heavens and on Earth.

MANZAL LAZI YASHFAOO INDAHU ILLA BE-IZNIHI

Who is there can intercede in His presence except as He permitteth?

YA'LAMU MA BAINA AYDEEHIM WAMA KHALFAHUM

He knoweth what (appeareth to His creatures as) before or after or behind them.

WALA YUHEETOONA BISH-EY-IM MIN ILMIHI ILLA BIMA SHA'A

Nor shall they compass aught of His knowledge except as He willeth.

WASIYA KURSI-US-SAMAWATE WALARDH

His Throne doth extend over the heavens and the earth,

WALA YA'OODOHU HIFZUHUMA

and He feeleth no fatigue in guarding and preserving them.

WA HUWAL ALIYUL AZEEM

for He is the Most High, the Supreme (in glory)."

It is reported from Abu Huraira that the Prophet had said, "In Sura Baqara there is a verse that is master of all verses. Whoever has Shaitan in his house and he recites it, he (Shaitan) will leave his house. That verse is the verse of the throne (*ayat al kursi*).

Another prayer is the one that was used by the Prophet during the Meraj incident mentioned above. When he was pursued by a Jinn who came after him with a burning flame (something we are recognizing as the jet wash from an afterburner) the Prophet spoke the following words:

A'OOZU BI WAJUHILLAHI KAREEMI WABI KALIMATILLAH-I-TAMMA TALLATI LA YUJAWIZUHUNNA BARRUNWALA FAJIRUMIN SHARRIMA YANZILU MINASSAMA-I WAMIN SHARRIMA YA'RUJU FIHA WAMIN SHARRIMA ZARA 'A FIL ARDI WAMINSHARI MA YAKHRUJ MINHA WAMAN FITANIL LAILI WANNAHARE WAMANE TAWAR-I-LAYLE WANNAHAR-I-LA TARIQAN YATRUQU BIKHAIRINYA RAHMAN.

"I seek refuge in Allah's glory and position, through his (taught) utterances, from the evil that descends from the skies or ascends thereon. For no one amongst them can subjugate these utterances. And from the evil of all that enters and leaves the earth, and from the mischief makers of the day and the night. And from the stealers of the night and of the day, except those who deliver good oh merciful."

CHAPTER 8

IN ALLIANCE WITH THE DEVIL

Islamic Perspective on UFO Cover-up

As previously classified UFO documents become available to the general public, what also comes into view is a global censorship plan by which all information leading to the UFO phenomenon was systematically censored. The U.S. government has been accused of repeatedly engaging in an unnecessary and unjustified attempt to conceal this information from the world. UFO literature produced by the West presents a number of "cover-up theories" attempting to explain why the American government has hidden this highly crucial and sensitive information from the world. These "cover-up theories" range from being somewhat convincing to downright ridiculous and covering every spectrum in between. The most commonly accepted cover-up theories in the West are:

- Concealment of information regarding all forms of flying objects was/is necessary to protect the secrecy of experimental military aircraft being developed in the United States.

- Any official acknowledgment of intelligent extraterrestrial life will cause a war, nerves, and mass hysteria throughout the world. The masses are not ready to accept the idea, as it does not fit into our present worldview.
- Contact has been established with aliens and the U.S. government is already exchanging technology with them. The deal has to be kept top secret because any compromise on the secrecy of such an agreement compromises the national security of the world's only existing super power.

These theories, no matter how vague or simplistic, have convinced the vast majority of UFO believers of their existence because all three of the above explanations tend to suggest that the government is acting in the interest of the people. "We are being deceived for our own benefit."

Once we recognize the connection between Quranic Jinns and UFOs, a new picture unfolds, and we begin to understand the real reason why UFO-related information has been withheld from the world. The real reason is far more frightening than the human mind is willing to accept. Before we get into the reasons for the UFO cover-up, I would like to spend a portion of this chapter highlighting the debate that has gone on in the United Nations over the concealment of UFO-related information by the United States.

Cover-up in the United Nations

On December 18, 1978, UFOs were finally on the official agenda of the United Nations (UN). Proposal 33/426 called for the immediate establishment of a department within the United Nations that would research the issue of UFOs and disseminate the related information. The proposal called for the member states to investigate unexplained aerial phenomenon in their own countries and forward the results to the United Nations. It was also suggested that the United Nations Committee on Peaceful Uses of Outer Space (UN-CPUOS) should take specific steps in the matters related to UFOs. Surprisingly, the proposal was accepted by the plenary session, but the UN did not act according to it and almost none of the proposed activities were implemented.[108]

It still remains a mystery why, after its acceptance, Proposal 33/426 was ignored. Officials who had the opportunity to observe the situation closely spoke of a conspiracy by the United States to prevent the formation of such a department. They accused the United States of doing everything behind the scenes to obstruct the development of such a lobby. Most of this criticism came from a UN employee named Maj. Colmon S. Von Keviczky.

Col. Colmon S. Von Keviczky was an officer in the Public Information's Office of the UN. He had a master's degree in Military Sciences and Engineering from Royal Hungarian Maria Ludovika Military Academy, and had two years of training in film production from UFA Motion Picture Academy in Berlin. For seven years he served in the Hungarian Army as the chief of the Audio-Visual Department of the General Staff and Defense Ministry, but during the Soviet Invasion

---

[108] Hesseman, p. 425

of Hungary, he fled to Germany from where the U.S. Army employed him as a camera operator.

In 1952, when he came to the United States, his attention was drawn for the very first time to UFOs. Being an expert in film and still camera photography, he analyzed a great deal of UFO-related visual material and came to the conclusion that some very serious and solid photographic evidence was being ignored by the Pentagon.

During his term in the UN Public Information Office, he sent to U Thant, the Secretary General of United Nations at the time, a memorandum consisting of 124 UFO-related documents. The Secretary found the material so interesting that on February 9, 1966, he invited Von Keviczky to his office for a personal discussion on the subject. During this discussion, it was decided that the UN would work on the development of an agency whose purpose would be to try to establish contact with the visitors. Von Keviczky himself was to lay out the plan for such a project. Furthermore, the Secretary General contacted another supporter of the UFO theory, Prof. James McDonald of the University of Arizona to address the UN-CPUOS on the subject.

On June 27, 1967, a news heading appeared in the *New York Post*, which stated that next to the war in Vietnam, U Thant con- sidered UFOs to be the next biggest challenge for the United Nations! The news was followed by an immediate intervention by both super- powers. Nikolai Trofimirovich Federenko, the Soviet Ambassador to the UN, declared UFOs to be the "nightmare of imperialistic and capitalistic nations" while the United States tried to convince the Secretary General that the task should be given to a bigger university and, surprisingly, it was the University of Colorado that was selected for the project. In the days that followed, Von Keviczky was removed from his post. He was told that his employment within the UN had been terminated under pressure from the United States.[109]

In April 1977, Prime Minister of Grenada Sir Eric Gairy was invited to speak at a UFO congress in Acapulco, Mexico. He addressed his gathering as follows:

"In the same way that this planet is the accepted inheritance of all humanity, knowledge is also to be shared for the benefit of all mankind, and in this light one wonders why the existence of UFOs or flying saucers, as they are sometimes called, continues to remain a secret to those in whose archives repose useful information and other data. While we appreciate that some countries consider this to be in the interest of military expedience, I now urge a different view be taken because it is my firm belief that the world is ready, willing, and mature enough to accept these phenomenon." [110]

Mysteries of Area 51

About one hundred miles north of Las Vegas lays Groom Lake, Nevada, one of the most inhospitable and remote places on this planet. The lone road that goes to the dry lake passes through a barren desert and carries warning signs on both sides that tell an approaching driver that he is not welcomed where he is heading; that he is approaching a place where the use of lethal force is

[109] Hesseman, pp. 454-456
[110] Hesseman, pp. 459-460

authorized; where trespassers will be killed, etc. There cannot be a more sinister place than this. Today, the mention of Groom Lake has been deleted from all recent maps, but older maps used to refer to the region as "Area 51."

For the last fifty years, Area 51 has been the testing area for the world's most secret fighter aircrafts. U-2, A-12, SR-71, and F-117 Stealth were all test flown in this region years before they came into public view. The facility was built in the 1950s under the supervision of the CIA when the spot qualified as the most remote location in the United States. Upon completion, its mention was removed from all maps and the U.S. government refuses to acknowledge its existence. Mysterious security personnel with no identification badges guard the place, and it is well known that they have the orders to kill any trespassers.

What goes on at this base is so secret that even the employees who work there do not know what they are working on. They are only allowed to talk to people to whom they directly report, and it is known that before a test flight is carried out and aircraft is taken out of its hangar, the ground crew are given orders to lie down on their chests with their faces buried in the ground and not look up until the aircraft has flown off. Once it is out of sight, they can get up and carry about their business. They are to follow the same procedure while the testing plane returns for landing. Thus, people have worked there for years without actually looking at what is being test flown there.

As previously classified UFO documents emerge, it has been said that this top secret military facility, which is spread over an area of 12,500 square miles (bigger than the country of Belgium with more than 1/3ʳᵈ of it being restricted space) is not only the home of experimental military aircrafts, but also another kind of technology that the world does not know about—alien flying saucers! It has been argued that the flying saucer that crashed in Roswell, New Mexico is stored in Area 51.

On November 6, 1989, an exclusive interview was broadcasted on KLAS-TV in Las Vegas and the subject was a thirty-one-year-old scientist named Bob Lazar. On public television, Lazar claimed that he was hired by the U.S. government to do research work in Area 51. His job in the most secret military facility in the world was to back-engineer a UFO. He stated that the U.S. Air Force had in its possession not one, but nine such discs and top U.S. scientists had been studying their propulsion system for forty years. Out of nine, two were damaged and the rest of the seven were intact. The technology was so complicated that it had only been a decade since they gained a basic understanding of their principles.[111]

Lazar went on to explain how the flying saucers were powered. It was not based on the principles of action and reaction, but on reverse magnetism! When it started, its underside would glow. It would hiss like a sphere loaded with high voltage current. That also explained why the discs were round. Insulators of high voltage systems are made rounded so that a coronal, all-round discharge is possible. Lazar also talked about an anti-matter reactor with a chip of element 115. When bombarded with protons, element 115 would

---

[111] Hesseman, pp. 371-372

change, disintegrate, and set the anti-matter and gravity waves free. Wave conductors and gravity amplifiers were then used to channel the waves to build a gravitational field around the craft.[112]

Not only was Lazar describing new flight principles, his theory of anti-matter seemed to explain the impossible flight character-istics of UFOs never understood previously by UFO experts. G-forces had been one of the greatest mysteries of UFO flight. How could the occupants twist and turn in the air at enormous speeds without having the G-force affect them? Lazar's explanation seemed to explain that since the ship was capable of producing its own gravity, the occupants were not subjected to any external G-force. It also explained why navigational instruments and compasses on planes went crazy when a UFO flew close to them. Furthermore, element 115 does not occur on Earth, nor can it be made synthetically. Synthetic elements reach the level of 92 on the periodic table, and above 103 and higher than plutonium, they disintegrate too fast. Scientists had speculated that elements 113 to 116 would again be stable and element 115 that Lazar was describing confirmed that. The U.S. government, according to Lazar, had over five hundred pounds of this element. It was extremely heavy and had to be transported in laden chests.[113]

All indications showed that Lazar was genuine, for he was giving out information about the crafts that seemed to match perfectly with the observed UFO behavior. Regarding the secrecy of Area 51, Lazar

---

[112] Hesseman, p. 373

[113] Hesseman, pp. 373-374

said that that was one of the reasons why he gave up his job. He had no privacy; he was watched all the time. His phone calls were monitored and he was again and again reminded of his oath of secrecy. He also stated that the armed personnel threatened him with their weapons telling him that he would die if he talked about his secret project with anyone outside.

When a background check was done on Lazar, it turned out that the man did not exist. The university that he claimed he had attended denied enrolling any such individual. The Los Alamos lab where he claimed to have worked before his assignment in Area 51 also denied having employed any such person. Almost none of his previous records could be found. Lazar claimed that they were deleted later by intelligence agencies because he was disclosing sensitive information, and the agencies wanted to turn him into a nonexisting individual. They achieved that not by killing him, but by deleting all of his records.

Journalists did not give up on the case and, on further investigation and probing, what came out was an old, dusty copy of an internal telephone book belonging to the Los Alamos Lab. Lazar's name was clearly shown on the list of employees. It became clear that his employment and educational records had been deleted after he came out in public with the information.

Bob Lazar was not the only one to break the silence regarding Area 51. Similar revelations had come from a man within the intelligence, who chose to be identified only by his code name "Falcon." In "UFO Cover-up Live," which was broadcasted in the United States in 1988, Falcon appeared on TV and spoke from under a shadow with a mechanized voice. "Inside the MJ-12 community there is a book . . . This book, or as it is called within the MJ-12 community, 'the bible,' contains historically everything that has occurred from the Truman era up to the three aliens being guests of the United States government. It includes technological data gathered from the aliens, medical history gathered from the dead aliens that were found in the desert, autopsy information, and information gathered from the aliens about their social structure and the universe. Presently, as of the year 1988, there is one extraterrestrial being here as a guest of the United States government, and he is remained hidden from public view. The "Yellow Book" is a book that was exclusively written by the second extraterrestrial being. It contains information about the planet of the aliens, their solar system, their dual suns, their culture, their social makeup and structure, and their life among earthlings."[114]

Alien guests of the U.S. government? The idea seems too far-fetched to be true. But the background of "Falcon" has been verified by many people in the media, including CBS reporter Peter Leone. After doing a thorough check on Falcon, Leone stated, "It was possible for me to verify Falcon's credentials. In 1987, I met Falcon again and once more I was able to confirm his references. It became clear to me that he was what he claimed to be."

History of UFO Cover-up

UFO cover-up is not anything new. The priests of the ancient civilizations also concealed UFO-related information from their

---

[114] Hesseman, pp. 370-371

masses. In Sumerian, Mayan, Egyptian, and Hindu civilizations the secrets of the "gods" remained primarily within the priesthood. Masses believed in their mystical powers as they had seen these "holy men" call upon the gods and perform miracles for their worshippers. Both Egypt and Sumeria had libraries in which old secrets were preserved, taught, and learned. In *Chariots of Gods?* Von Daniken addresses this ancient prehistoric UFO cover-up with the following question:

> "Why are the oldest libraries in the world secret libraries? What are people really afraid of? Are they worried that the truth protected and concealed for so many thousands of years, will finally come to light?"[115]

These civilizations worshipped what would be called in Islamic (as well as Jewish and Christian) tradition, "Tribe of Iblees" or Shayateen (plural of Satan). Thus, they were devil worshippers. It is no coincidence that the rituals of some satanic cults bear such striking resemblance to the worship that was carried out in these ancient societies. Snake worship, fairly common in satanic cults, can also be seen in Hindu temples across India. Hindu villagers in India still fall on the ground and lay prostrate at the sight of a King Cobra. Historical wall paintings in Egypt depict pharaohs wearing crowns with cobra heads and carrying staffs that resemble snakes. Of the Mayan civilization, Erich Von Daniken wrote:

> "The snake is a symbol of nearly all Mayan buildings. That is astonishing; for one would have expected a people surrounded by

---

[115] Von Daniken, p. 44

luxuriant rampant flora to leave flower motifs behind on their stone reliefs as well. Yet, the loathsome snake confronts us everywhere. From time immemorial the snake has wound its way through the dust and dirt of the earth. Why should anyone conceive of endowing it with the ability to fly? Being the primeval image of evil, the snake is condemned to crawl. How could anyone worship this repulsive creature as a god, and why would it fly into the bargain? Among the Mayans it could."[116]

We can call these ancient civilizations "Satanists" or "alien worshippers," but Prophet Muhammad used a very interesting term to refer to them; he called these ancient peoples, as well as pagan Arabs, "Kafirs!" Interestingly, the literal meaning of the word *kafir* is, "the one who conceals or withholds information!" A very fitting name for alien worshippers, isn't it? Furthermore, Prophet Muhammad declared that, like Moses, Abraham, Jesus, and all other Prophets, his mission was also to eradicate *Kufr* (concealment) from the world. Was he talking about eradicating concealment of alien contact? Let's see. Islamic history tells us that two years before his death, the Prophet's army marched on the city of Mecca. After surrounding the city by four sides, the army of ten thousand closed in. The streets and bazaars of Mecca became deserted as people locked themselves in their houses in terror. Instead of mass killing and looting, which had been a standard ritual for a conquering army, the Prophet led his men straight to the Kaaba. At the time, this was the cube-shaped structure that housed hundreds of alien astronauts

[116] Von Daniken, p. 125

carved out of wood or hewn from stone. *The Concise Encyclopedia of Islam* describes the idols as follows:

"Apart from astral deities representing cosmic principles inherited from Mesopotamians[117], many gods were Ba'ls like those of the Old Testament and totems of particular tribes." [118]

Astral deities? The most celebrated of these cosmic gods were Hubal (God of the moon), Uzza, a female goddess worshipped in different parts of Arabia, and the Sun god Munaaf.[119]

Islamic history further tells us that the Prophet opened the small door and with a wooden staff in his hand, entered the Kaaba. "The truth is here and 'cover-up' has been eliminated!" he announced loudly as he brought the astronaut gods down to the floor one after another with the wooden staff. The exact word that the Prophet used for cover-up was "baatil." The Prophet was reciting the Quranic verse, Sura 17:81.

017.081. And say: "Truth has (now) arrived, and Falsehood perished: for Falsehood is (by its nature) bound to perish."

Most English translations of the Quran have mistranslated the word "baatil" as "falsehood." The literal meaning of the word is "concealment" or more accurately, "cover-up." Later on, the Prophet used his sword to cut open some of these fallen idols and black smoke arose from out of them; this was a sign of a psychic influence that the statues generated on their followers. In *The Concise*

---

[117] Mesopotamians were the same people as Sumerians.
[118] Glasse, p. 179
[119] Cyril Glasse, p. 179

Encyclopedia of Islam, Cyril Glasse continues to write, "Thus the attraction the idols exerted over their devotees was not arbitrary, but the result of a projected psychic influence; to this in return the worshipper could respond."

The Prophet died two years after the elimination of cover-up from Mecca. His political successors, the Caliphs, took over his place with the same political objective, i.e., the elimination of kufr (cover-up) from the world. On the orders of the first Caliph, Khalid bin Waleed took 10,000 men and marched northwards to Mesopotamia (Iraq), the land of Sumerians. Within a year of the Prophet's death, Iraq fell to Muslims and Kufr (concealment) was abolished from the region.

Yet, even after its conquest, the area remained intense with UFO activity. When the second Caliph, Umar bin Al Khattab, decided to visit what was once the land of Sumerians, he was warned of an alien presence in the region. Kaab bin Ahbar, one of the Caliph's companions, advised: "O' leader of the faithful, do not go there (Iraq), for 90 percent of the place is infested with magic; there is presence of evil Jinns and the land has troublesome epidemics."[120]

The universal war against cover-up (Kufr) continued and in the next few years, Egypt, another land of these astronaut deities, was overrun. It was a hundred years later that the Muslim armies lead by Muhammad bin Qasim had breached into Hindu India with their objective to eliminate UFO concealment!

---

[120] Suyooti, p. 104

Munafiqeen

During these years between the sixth and ninth century, Muslim scholars did ample research on the alien visitors whose worship they were eradicating from the planet. All forms of alien contact, from demonic possession to phantom pregnancies, were investigated and legislations were made in Islamic Shariah law regarding human contact with these beings. By the end of the ninth century, Imam Jalal-ud-din Sayooti, a scholar from Cairo, compiled his famous volume, *The History of Jinns and Devils*; portions of which read like any modern paperback on alien contact.

While this academic, political, and military struggle continued against global UFO cover-up, not all people in the converted lands of Mesopotamia and Egypt had given up alien worship. Some had undergone false Islamic conversions and practiced their occult rituals in secret. Mainstream Muslims referred to them as hypocrites (*Munafiqee*n). They would be Muslims in public, but in the privacy of their secret gatherings they continued with their occult rituals. They would utter "mantras" or code words to call upon the gods that their ancestors worshipped. The gods would come and aid them.

While Muslim majority shunned these practices, the sorcery of the Munafiqeen still fascinated them. It was this fascination with the Munafiqeen that became the major selling point for *Tales of the Arabian Nights*. In *Aladdin and the Magic Lamp*, the story revolves around a boy who uses his alliance with a Jinn to commit theft, abduct people, and teleport objects from place to place. His alien connection not only rewards him with riches, but also enables him to operate outside the laws that society had set for itself.

In his compilation of Islamic rulings, Ahmed Ibn Tamiyeh wrote about the Munafiqeen:

"People of misguidance and heresies, those who are ascetic and worshippers but not according to the shariah, sometimes have a strong influence that draws many to the places of Satan in which it is prohibited to pray. This is because the devils descend upon them and the devils talk to them about some matters the same way they talk to fortune tellers. In the same manner, they enter the statues and idols and talk to the worshippers of the idols. They help them in some of their needs in the same manner they help magicians. In the same manner, they help the worshipper of idols, the sun, the moon and the planets when they worship them in the manner they think that are deserving of, of sanctifying them, to dressing and lighting incense for them and so on. Devils, that they call "*spirits of the planets*", descend upon them and meet some of their needs.[121]

Knights Templars

The story of Knights Templars is an interesting one. It was during the Crusades that the Western world got its hands on the secrets of UFO worship practiced by the Munafiqeen. As we see in this chapter, when Crusading armies returned to Europe, some knights also took with them the forbidden secrets of establishing alien contact. Upon

---

[121] Ahmed Ibn Tamiyah, Majomoo, vol. 19, p. 41

finding out about these rituals, the Catholic Church hunted the alien worshippers all over Europe and burned them in public for the practice of black magic and devil worship. The trial and execution of these alien worshippers has been one of the most controversial trials in European history.

After the first Crusade, in the year 1118, a knightly order was established in Jerusalem whose objective was to guard the travel routes of the pilgrims. These knights, bound by monastic vows, became known as Knights Templars. While they had been assigned the duty of guarding pilgrims, they became more interested in the forbidden knowledge of the Munafiqeen. They began to seek the secrets of alien worship that was shunned both by Muslim and Christians.

It is not clear who gave the Templars the secrets of alien contact, but historians indicate it was a group of Munafiqeen called "Ashashin." Being a deviant offshoot of the Ismailis, the Ashashin were political murderers by profession. Armed with poisonous daggers they would mingle with local population and follow their targets till they were in striking range. Once close enough, they would strike the targeted individual without considering consequences of arrest or death. It was these very people that inspired the English word "assassins."

In the eleventh century Middle East, a great number of Muslim princes and officers had been struck down by their daggers. The earliest description of this cult comes from a report from an envoy of Emperor Frederick Barbarossa. The envoy that returned from Egypt and Syria described the Ashashin as follows:

"This breed of men lives without law; they eat swine's flesh against the laws of Saracens and make use of all women without distinction, including their mothers and sisters."[122]

In 1152, the Assassins murdered Raymond, Comte de Tripole of the Templars. In retaliation, the Templars moved into their territory and forced them into signing a treaty by which they were to pay the knights 12,000 gold pieces as expiation for their crime. During this time however, the Templars not only acquired from the Assassins their gold, but also the secrets of establishing alien contact. Dr. Brussel in his book, *Religious Thought and Heresy in the Middle Ages* states that they (Templars) had "long and important dealings" with the Assassins and were therefore "suspected (not unfairly) of imbibing their precepts and following their principles." [123]

The Crusades was a time of great political tension between the two religions. Among the ranks of the Crusaders, Knight's Templars were often admired by a fanatical hatred for Muslims. Furthermore, they had made certain incursions into Muslim lands for which they were looked upon by the rest of the Crusaders. The Pope took them under his immediate protection and they became immune to all authority, and answerable to no one except the Pope. Their property was exempted from all taxations even from the ecclesiastical tithes. Thus, in the next few years, the Templars amassed a great amount of wealth and evolved from a militant religious order to a powerful, economic lobby.

---

[122] Lewis, p. 2
[123] Bussell, pp. 796, 797

The defeat of the Crusaders came at the hands of Sallah-ud-din Ayubi (a.k.a. Saladin). In a decisive battle fought along the hills of Hattin, the main Crusader army lead by King Guy was defeated and most of the Latin leadership was taken prisoner. While Sallah-ud-din had a reputation of treating Christians with kindness, Templars were treated quite differently. Over two hundred of them were to be put to death. Even a humane figure like Sallah-ud-din, known all over the Christian world for his gentleness and chivalry, could not excuse the Templars. While a few were pardoned after converting to Islam, the rest (estimated to be 230) were executed.[124]

It was known that by the end of the Crusades, Templars had their headquarters in almost every country across Europe. During the Crusades, they had amassed such wealth that now they began to exert enormous influence on the countries that they returned to. They were financing nations and loaning money to the kings. It is also held by some historians that it was the Templars who developed banking as we know it today. Since interest was frowned upon by Christians as much as by Muslims, the Templars changed the manner in which the loans were paid back and were able to avoid the charge of usury. Thus, they multiplied their wealth to enormous proportions and were soon in the position to finance kings.

The demise of the Templars came in 1307 at the hands of the Pope and the king of France. Rumors regarding their bizarre rituals were already circulating and the secrecy with which they lived aroused the curiosity of many in powerful political circles. Finally,

---

[124] Nicolle, p, 79

King Philip the Fair could no longer remain indifferent to their activities and ordered an official inquiry. "There was reason to believe," said the king, "that the [Templar] order was profoundly heretical; that its military monks, in fact, were black magicians!" On Friday October 13, 1307, orders were issued to arrest all Templars and to present them in for an examination. This day became known as Friday the 13th and would be remembered all over Europe as a day symbolizing bad luck and misfortune.

The official accusations against the Templars were as follows:

The initiation ritual of the Templars required the new member to deny Christ, spit on the cross, and utter obscenities.

From that day on, they were to worship an idol named "Baphomet." Some historians have argued that this was a bearded head that was a distortion of the face of the Prophet Muhammad. Others argue the striking similarity in the pronunciation of Mahomet and Baphomet is a coincidence, and Baphomet was, in fact, a demonic head symbolizing an occult deity. The latter seems to be more likely, because except for the striking similarity of the pronunciation of Mahomet and Baphomet, there is no evidence to suggest that the idol symbolized a distortion of the Prophet of Islam.

Sodomy, homosexuality, and abnormal sexual rituals.

During the investigations, a great number of knights along with Jacques du Molay, the head of the Templars, declared themselves guilty to the charges. On May 12, 1310, fifty-four knights were burned alive at the stake. Four years later, the head of the Templars was burned in front of the city gates of Notre Dame.

Other nations in Europe were following the same course of action and right after the arrest of Jacques du Molay, Knight's

Templars were sought all over Europe, arrested, and tried. Those found innocent were given the choice to either serve under other military orders or to return to the secular state. Their wealth was seized, given to another military order called "The Hospitallers," and put to its original use (guarding the holy places).

The trial and burnings of the Templars has remained a controversial episode in European History. Historians sympathetic to the Templars have argued that there was no "occult" connection. It was said that the confessions of devil worship and sorcery were extracted under torture and that the Templars were crushed because their growing wealth and enormous political influence had started to threaten nations.

While it's a fact that torture was used in some trials and the growing economic/political influence of the Templars may have been a contributing factor in their suppression, there is enough evidence to show that the Templars were alien worshippers and self-proclaimed occultists.

Their contact with the Munafiqeen (Assassins) is well-documented in history. It is also documented that during the Crusades they adopted certain rituals and principles from the Assassins.

It is an undisputed fact that the Templars operated from within an uncompromising curtain of secrecy. They kept their rituals and meetings hidden from the public. If they were just "money lenders" why was the cloak of secrecy needed?

Though there is no evidence that they practiced incest like the Ashashin among mainstream Christianity, they were believed to be sexual deviants.

There is a striking resemblance in the Baphomet charge that

they were accused of and the idol worship that was carried out by the Munafiqeen.

While torture was used in some Christian countries, Templars admitted to the same charges even in countries where torture was not sanctioned.

Was the order destroyed because the church and the entire Christendom feared their growing wealth? Or was there another reason for their persecution? Manly P. Hall explains:

"It was not the physical power of the Templars, but the knowledge which they had brought with them from the East that the church feared."

He further adds: "They (Templars) had become wise in those mysteries which had been celebrated in Mecca thousands of years before the advent of Mohammed; they had read a few pages from the dread book of the anthropos, and for this knowledge they were doomed to die." [125]

Freemasonry: The Occult Origins

After their persecution in Europe, some Templars escaped to Scotland. In his book *The Holy Cross and Grail*, Michael Bradley explains:

"It is known that the Templars fled to Scotland, too, after the dissolution of 1312, and it is known that some found refuge among the Saint-Clairs of Rosslyn in Midlothian. There is a Templar cemetery there."

Since the term "Templar" was associated with occultism and devil worship, they had to operate under a different name.

---

[125] Monteith, p. 126

They started calling themselves Freemasons!

Over the last seven centuries, Freemasonry has emerged as a global order that recruits people from all across the world. Masonic scholars, who deny any occult connection, have given various definitions for their order. The world-renowned Masonic scholar Albert Pike explains, "Freemasonry is the subjugation of the human that is in man by the divine; the conquest of the appetites and passions by the moral sense and the reason; a continual effort, struggle, and warfare of the spiritual against the material and sensual."[126] Others have stated, "It seeks to guide the moral and spiritual development of humanity outside and above any differences of class, nationality, or creed . . . Its aims are the search for truth, the study of morality, and the practice of solidarity." [127]

Why then do they have the blood oaths, the secrecy, and the bizarre initiations? A great deal of material is available on the bizarre initiations practiced by Freemasonry.

Initiations

Upon arriving at the Masonic Temple, one finds himself in front of a locked door. A small window on top of the door will open and a head will peek out. The newly arrived must ask for an appointment.

When he visits the lodge again at that specified time, a spiritual guide receives him at the door. He is lead into a dark chamber called the "meditation room." Here he sees large temples, skulls, copper

---

[126] Albert Pike, p. 854
[127] El Amin, p. 111

snakes, and bones of human beings (mostly forearms and thighs). He is then made to bare one side of his chest and remove all metal from his body, including jewelry and wristwatches. "Are you still determined to the pursuit of the Freemasonic light?" The guide will ask. When the applicant says "yes" he will be blindfolded with a black cloth and a cord will be put around his neck.

The spiritual guide then leads the person to the door of the closed temple. After knocking, a guard from inside asks, "Who is it?" The spiritual guide replies, "A poor applicant in a state of darkness; he had applied for admission to Freemasonry voluntarily. He is now coming to acquire the light from this august lodge."

"In what hopes?" the voice from the inside will ask.

"In good conduct and free descent," the spiritual guide answers.

The door opens and the "applicant" is lead into the chamber of the chief. Still blindfolded, the guards make him walk around in twisted paths. Then, the applicant is made to stand between two posts and the chief will ask him questions. He will be told, "You are audaciously approaching a rigorous test and you will swear to your Holy Book by your honor and conscience, and you must sign with the ink of your blood. Are you still determined? You have sufficient time for thinking and you have a right to withdraw before taking an oath."

If the applicant answers in a yes, he will be given a glass of sweet water followed by a glass of bitter water. "The life of the human being is also exposed to bitterness; you must be satisfied to be happy," the chief says.[128]

---

[128] Amini and Habib, pp. 20-23

The Blood Oath

The oath taking begins with the applicant's hand being rubbed with soil. He will be made to kneel on his left knee, and he will place his hand on the Holy Book. Christians swear on the Gospel, Jews on the Old Testament, and Muslims on the Quran. Their Holy Scripture is placed on a podium and on top of this a compass and an angle are placed.[129] The applicant then swears on his book that he will always guard the secrets that will be revealed to him from time to time and that he takes upon himself "not to write them, nor to print them, nor to carve them, nor engrave them, nor show the way to them in any manner." He goes on to swear that he is binding himself "under no less penalty than that of having my throat cut across, my tongue torn out by its roots, and my body buried in the rough sands of the sea at low water mark where the tide ebbs and flows twice in twenty four hours, should I ever knowingly violate this, my entered apprentice obligation, so help me God . . ."[130]

After the oath he is told:

"Your stay in the darkness has lasted long. The society with which you are trying to be affiliated may cost you the last drops of your blood. Are you still determined to be affiliated?" If he still replies yes. He is asked, "What do you wish now?"

"Light," he answers.

"Let light be given to him," the chief responds.

---

[129] Amini and Habib, p. 23

[130] Monteith, p. 119

The moment the cover from the applicant's eyes is removed, he sees drawn swords aimed at his face and at his heart.

"These swords are for your defense at need, as well as to slay you if you act treacherously toward your pledges, agreements, and oaths. This cord, which is around your neck, is to choke you if you take an action or to manifest a sign which indicates violation of the oaths. Seconds ago you were foreign to our kinsfolk and we had been addressing you as "Oh applicant," but now you have become a Freemasonic brother, your right is as all the brothers rights and your duty as theirs."[131]

This day of consecration is considered in Freemasonry as one's true birthday. Masons do not ask "What is your degree?" or "How long have you been in the brotherhood." Instead they ask, "What is your age?" [132]

There are thirty-three degrees in Masonry and every time a member advances to a higher degree, blood oaths are taken with similar ceremonies. Upon entering the Fellow Craft or the second degree, he agrees to have his . . . breast torn open, my heart plucked out, and given as a prey to the birds of the air and the beasts of the field . . .[133]

In the third degree, he binds himself under the penalty of having "my body cut into two, my bowels taken from thence and burned to ashes, and the ashes scattered to the four winds of the heaven, that

---

[131] Amini and Habib, p. 23
[132] Amini and Habib, p. 27
[133] Monteith, p. 119

no trace or remembrance may be had of so vile and perjured a wretch as I."[134]

In the thirteenth degree, the Mason agrees to "keep exactly in my heart all the secrets that shall be revealed to me. And in failure of this my oath, I consent to have my body opened perpendicularly and to be exposed for eight hours in the open air that the venomous flies may eat of my intestines, my head to be cut off and to be put on the highest pinnacle of the world, and I will always be ready to inflict the same punishment on those who shall disclose this degree and break this oath."[135]

In the twenty-eighth degree, he says, "May my brethren seize me and thrust my tongue through with red iron, to pluck off my eyes to deprive me of smelling and seeing, to cut off my hands and expose me in that condition in the field to be devoured by the voracious animals, and if none can be found, may the lightening of heaven execute on me the same vengeance."[136]

Once in the order, Masons help their fellow Masons move into positions of power and influence. They plant their men into important positions across the world in governments, the military, and mass media. Some of the most important people in recent history have been Freemasons. General Douglas MacArthur (legendary general of the Second World War), Winston Churchill (British Prime Minister during the Second World War), Benjamin Franklin (American printer, author, scientist, philosopher and

---

[134] Monteith, p. 119

[135] El-Amin, p. 113

[136] El Amin, p. 113

diplomat), Napoleon Bonaparte (French Emperor), and Mustufa Kemal Ataturk (Turkish nationalist reformer) were all Freemasons. At least five of the last twelve American presidents were Masons. The sixth one was a member of DeMolays, a Masonic club for boys. Known Masons in the entertainment industry include Hollywood actors John Wayne, Clark Gable, Oliver Hardy (of the Laurel and Hardy comedic duo), and the creator of Sherlock Holmes, Sir Arthur Conan Doyle.

Cecil John Rhodes, the founder of Zimbabwe was a Freemason. He was known for his diamond mining operations all over Africa. In his book *Confessions of Faith* he wrote about his bizarre rituals.

"I see the wealth and power they possess, the influence they hold, I think over their ceremonies, and I wonder that a large body of men can devote themselves to what at times appears the most ridiculous and absurd rites without an object and without an end."[137]

Masonic Network is an international one. All over the world they help their men move into positions of wealth and influence. They also have a significant following in the Muslim world. In Turkey, for example, in the year 1882, there were approximately 10,000 Freemasons. Among them were ministers, representatives, army commanders, and senior public officials. A Freemasonic lodge was founded in Turkey patterned after the grand orient of France. Its name was later changed to the "Committee of Union and Progress." One of the prominent members of this establishment was Mustafa Kemal (Ataturk) the founder of "Secular Turkey." As an entrenched

---

[137] Monteith, p. 117

Freemason, he declared that Islam, the religion dedicated to uprooting UFO cover-up from the world, is nothing more than rules and reflections of an Arab Sheikh.[138]

In Karachi, Pakistan, opposite the Pakistan International Airlines Office, is an old white building. The board on it reads "Society for the Preservation of Wildlife." Once in the compound we see an old staircase leading upstairs to the second floor. There are Masonic plaques on both sides of the staircase, and they bear the names of Pakistani Freemasons.

The office of Society for Preservation of Wildlife was a Masonic lodge during the end and was later shut down by the government of Pakistan. People of Karachi still refer to the building as the meeting place for Akhwan-ul-Shayateen. Masonry is also believed to have recruits in Egypt, Syria, Indonesia, Malaysia, and Thailand. As always, these are in influential positions in governments, ruling elite, the military, intelligentsia, and mass media.

In most cases when people join Freemasonry, they do not know what they are becoming part of. They know that they will be among chosen elite and their generations will be rewarded with wealth and influence. Once in the order, they have to help their "brethren under the secrecy of blood oaths." For this, they often go against the laws of the societies they are operating in. As they move to higher degrees they realize that this is not just an elitist club, but an occult organization whose rituals have been guarded for centuries. At that moment, they know they cannot break away from the order because

---

[138] Amini and Habib, p. 91

Masonry is capable of leaking the proof of their crimes. Furthermore, within the ranks of Masonry they have power and prestige and the ability to operate outside the law. The order gives them everything they need. The natural psychological dynamic in such a situation is to reconstruct one's own perception of right and wrong to suit their needs.

Illuminati and the Bonesmen

In 1786, the Bavarian government published a document called "The Original Writings of the Order and Sect of the Illuminati." The copies of this document were sent to churches and heads of states all across Europe. A year earlier, in 1785, the Bavarian government had launched a massive crackdown on an occult group that called itself Illuminati (i.e., illuminated ones or the light bearers). From the confiscated documents, it became apparent that the group was founded on May 1, 1776, by Dr. Adam Weishaupt, a professor of cannon law at the Ingolstadt University in Bavaria.[139] The aim of the organization was the global destruction of organized religion, elimination of ruling governments, and the establishment of a totalitarian rule under one world authority. The Illuminati referred to this as "Novus Ordo Seclorum" (The New Secular Order). The plan was to be accomplished by dividing the population of the world into opposing camps on political, economic, social, and other factors. The opposing elements were then to be armed and incidents were to be caused that would function as "triggers" to larger conflicts.

---

[139] Monteith, p. 56

The order was set up to pursue these goals on a long-term basis. Normally, conspirators try to achieve their objective within their lifetime, but this was not the case with the Illuminati. They had planned to recruit members for centuries from every coming generation until their political goal of the New World Order was met. The group had unlimited wealth at its disposal, for it was funded by Moses Amschel Bauer, who later came to be known as Nathan Rothschild, the father of international banking.

The activities of the Illuminati were uncovered in 1784 when Bavarian police launched a major crackdown closing the Grand Lodge of the Orient.[140] The incident became headline news of its time and the Bavarian government published the details of the conspiracy under the name "The Original Writings of the Order and the Sect of the Illuminati."

Though officially disbanded, the Illuminati continued to exist within Freemasonry. Seven years after the Bavarian crackdown on July 16, 1782, a meeting was held at the Congress of Wilhelmsbad. The details of this meeting are not fully known, but it is known that an alliance was sealed between Illuminati and the Freemasons, which united the two together and brought together no less than three million members across the world.

In the decades that followed, it was realized by the group that three large wars would have to be instigated that would pave the way for their New World Order. These wars were described in great detail by General Albert Pike, who was the top Illuminist in the

---

[140] Amini and Habib, p. 8

United States and the Sovereign Grand Commander of Scottish Rite of Freemasonry. In a letter addressed to Guisseppe Mazzini (dated August 15, 1871) Pike stated that the first war was to be initiated to end the Czarist regime in Russia and bring the land under the direct control of Illuminati agents. The second war, caused by manipulation of the differences between German Nationalists and political Zionists, was to end in the destruction of the first and the establishment of a Zionist state in Palestine. The third was to erupt from differences between Zionists and leaders of the Islamic world, in which one would destroy the other. The conflict was intended to spread worldwide and level the ground for the New World Order![141]

Almost half a century after Pike's letter, the First World War took place, Czarist Russia was destroyed, and Communism emerged as a new political force. Two decades later, the Second World War erupted and resulted in the destruction of Nazism and German nationalism. Three years after the war, Israel was established on land that originally belonged to the Arabs. The poison of this Arab-Israeli conflict is spreading around the world and the third war Pike described (between Zionism and Islam) is quite foreseeable.

Should Pike's letter to Mazzini be treated as a coincidence? Is it also a coincidence that to this very day, Communists celebrate their national holiday on May 1, the day that the Illuminati were created? Most people today do not know of Pike's letter or the Illuminati, but prior to 1930, the term Illuminati was well known. As Illuminists moved into positions of influence, their mention was removed from

---

[141] Amini and Habib, p. 13

all textbooks, encyclopedias, and dictionaries.[142] If anyone can get a copy of encyclopedia Britannica from the year 1901, he will find the term Illuminati listed there.

Some researchers maintain that the Illuminati exist even today. It exists in the United States under the name of Skull and Bones. The organization is known to operate from Yale University. For over 160 years, prominent families have sent their children to Yale to be inducted into the order. Every year, fifteen juniors are "tapped" by seniors to be initiated into the sect. After their initiation and rebirth, they become part of the ruling elite that operates outside the law. They are assured of prominent positions in life as the group is geared toward overall success of its members in their post-collegiate world. In its early days, the society held its meetings in hired halls, but a windowless hall was created in 1856 called "the tomb." This is where the initiations and occult rituals of Skull and Bones were carried out. Many Bonesmen have graduated from Yale and held important positions in politics, the military, industry, banking, and law.

When Jimmy Carter ran for the presidency in 1976 he promised, "If I become president, I will make every piece of information this country has about UFO sightings available to the public and the scientists." He became the president and in keeping his promise he released around 20,000 pages of classified UFO-related documents. In this, he encountered fierce opposition from certain lobbies within the government. He made a number of powerful enemies, one of whom was the Director of the CIA and later American President, George Bush.

---

[142] William Monteith, p. 57

Why would George Bush prevent Carter from releasing UFO-related information to Americans? The answer can be found in *Brotherhood of Darkness* by Dr. Stanley Monteith. What you are about to read is one of the most interesting extracts present in this book:

"All Bonesmen help their brethren advance into society. One example is the Bush family. Prescott Bush joined Skull and Bones in 1917; his son President George H. Bush was selected a generation later; his grandson Governor George W. Bush was inducted two generations later."[143]

Brotherhood of Darkness was published in the year 2000. Months after its publication, Governor George W. Bush ran for the presidency and after the most controversial election in the history of United States, became the president.

Conclusion

We have visitors! They have been coming since the very time of our origins. Ancient civilizations took them as gods and erected temples to their worship. The remains of these are scattered all over the world. In reference to these ancient alien worshippers, the Quran says:

> Say: "Travel through the earth and see what was the end of those before (you): Most of them worshipped other gods besides Allah." 30:42

Within these societies, there existed individuals who were in contact with the gods, and represented on the Earth an alien cause.

---

[143] William Montieth, p. 78

The gods rewarded them with advanced technology, which was perceived as magic by others. In *Bhagvata Purana*, we read that the devotees of the sky gods were given flying machines and that Lord Krsna used a sonar-guided missile to bring down an enemy called Vimana. It is well established today that a significant number of America's elite have been occultists. Should we really find it unbelievable that crashed discs and alien technology is being back-engineered in Area 51? What is so unbelievable about the idea that the gods who rewarded their ancient devotees with sound-seeking arrows (sonar-guided weapons) have given their present devotees F-117 stealth, B-2, and other aircrafts test flown in Area 51? The theory of top-secret military aircrafts being back-engineered from alien technology begins to make perfect sense.

These alien-human liaisons, which have been going on for thousands of years, are mentioned very clearly in the Quran:

006.128 YUSUFALI: One day will He gather them all together, (and say): "O ye assembly of Jinns! Much (toll) did ye take of men." *Their friends amongst men will say: "Our Lord! we made profit from each other*: but (alas!) we reached our term - which thou didst appoint for us." He will say: "The Fire be your dwelling-place: you will dwell therein for ever, except as Allah willeth." for thy Lord is full of wisdom and knowledge.

Ever wondered why the Pentagon, the military headquarters of the United States, is shaped like a star? Pentagram is an occult symbol used in demon worship and witchcraft. Is it really a coincidence that the military headquarters of the United States' armed forces is shaped like an occult emblem? Is it also a coincidence that in order to actually see the shape of the structure, one must look down upon it from the sky? When people on the ground are not capable of making out the shape of the five-pointed architecture, whom exactly is the colossal star shape meant for? The readers should bring to mind the ancient occult markings the Mayans left on the ground for the gods that came from the skies.

The secret societies that invisibly rule the world have left hidden clues to their existence. We see their signs all around us in our daily lives in magazines, books, architecture, national flags, and designer labels but do not recognize them as occult symbols. Every time you look at the back of a dollar bill you will see their emblem—a pyramid capped with an illuminated eye. Researchers who have studied occult symbols have pointed out that the pyramid and the glorified eye represent the Illuminati. Close to it we see in numbers, the date the Illuminati was created, May 1, 1776! The official explanation to the date is that May 1, 1776 was the day the American constitution was signed. What the official explanation does not explain is the line that is written right under it. The three words NOVUS ORDO SECLORUM! (The New Secular Order!)

It is well accepted that the French Revolution was sponsored by the Illuminati (the light bearers as the word means). After the revolutionaries seized power in France, they sent to the United States a gift that came loaded in ships. It was assembled in New York and stands today as a testimony to the French-American friendship. Thousands of tourists from all over the world have seen the Statue of Liberty, but haven't understood that what they are looking at is the "light bearer"—a symbol of the Illuminati.

Tomorrow's Islam

Islam is often portrayed as an old and rigid religion that is no longer compatible with the modern world. The truth is that Islam is the ideology of tomorrow. The Quran, the nucleus of Islam, was never "new" and can never become "old" because its source (God) lies outside of the dimensions of space and time. Muslim understanding of it, however, is primitive and needs to be updated.

It is quite foreseeable that in tomorrow's world there will only be two main ideologies. The first is the Secular Order, which has obvious roots in alien worship and Satanism. The second is Islam, which recognizes alien contact and considers its own objective to be the elimination of the UFO Cover-up (Kufr) from the world. In this global war of ideas, the latter will consume the former. May God give us all the wisdom to see the truth and the courage to accept it when we see it.

Note: Views expressed in this book belong to the author and not the news organizations the author has worked for.

Bibliography

Akram, Lt. Gen. A. I. *The Sword of Allah*. Rawalpindi: Army Education Press G.H.Q, 1970.

Blanch, Lesley. *The Sabres of Paradise*. London: John Murray (reprinted in Lahore by Combine Printers), 1960.

Bucaille, Maurice. *The Bible, the Quran, and Science*. (Publisher and date of publication unknown).

Bussell, F. W. *Religious Thought and Heresy in the Middle Ages*. Kennikat Press (date of publication unknown).

El-Amin, Mustufa. *Al Islam, Christianity, and Freemasonry*. New Jersey: New Mind Productions, 1985.

Glasse, Cyril. *Concise Encyclopedia of Islam*. New York: Harper San Francisco, 1989.

Hesseman, Michael. *UFOs the Secret History*. New York: Marlowe and Company, 1998.

Hoodbhoy, Pervez. *Islam and Science: Religious Orthodoxy and the Battle for Rationality*. London/New Jersey: Zed Books Ltd, 1991.

Jacobs, David M. *Secret Life*. New York: Simon and Schuster, 1992.

Kumar, Rajendra 'Rajiv'. *World Famous Discoveries*. New Delhi: Family Books Pvt. Ltd., 1992.

Lewis, Bernard. *The Assassins: A Radical Sect in Islam*. New York: Oxford University Press, 1967.

Monteith, William. *Brotherhood of Darkness*. Oklahoma City: Hearthstone Publishing, 2000.

Nicolle, David. *Hattin 1187*. Wellingborough, UK: Osprey Publishing, date unknown.

Phillips, Dr. Abu Ameenah Bilal. *The Exorcist Tradition in Islam*. Sharjah: UAE Dar Al Fatah Printing Publishing and Distribution Co. LLC, 1997.

Randles, Jenny. *The Complete Book of Aliens & Abductions*. London: Judy Paitkus (Publishers) Ltd., 1999.

Safwat, Muhammad as Saqqa Amini and Sa'di Abu Habib. *Freemasonry*. New York: Muslim World League Publications, 1982.

Sulaiman al-Ashqar, Dr. Umar. *The World of Jinns and Devils*. Boulder: Al Basheer Company for Publications and Translations, 1998.

Suyooti, Imam Jalaluddin. *Tareekh-e-Jinnat-0-Shayateen (History of Jinns and Devils)*. Urdu Translation by Maulana Imdadullah Anwer. Dar-ul-Muarif, Multan.

Thompson, Richard L. *Alien Identities*. San Diego: Govardhan Hill Inc., 1993.

Veliankode, Sidheeque M.A. *Doomsday: Portents and Prophecies*. Canada: Al-Attique Publishers Inc., 1999.

Von Daniken, Erich. *Chariots of the Gods?*. London/Canada: Souvenir Press Ltd., 1969.